Friends on the Way

Pete + Ali

with gratitude for your friendship
+ love

Maureen

Maureen Henderson

Friends on the Way

*A life enriched by engagement with
people of many faiths*

EPWORTH PRESS

0 7162 0529 7

First published 1999
by Epworth Press
20 Ivatt Way
Peterborough, PE3 7PG

Typeset by Regent Typesetting, London
Printed and bound in Great Britain by
Biddles Ltd, Guildford and King's Lynn

To the Community of the Sacred Passion
who shared the journey for thirty years and birthed me
into a wider community

Contents

Foreword

Maureen Henderson is a practitioner rather than a theorist. But her practical work, as a Christian committed to mission in a multifaith society, is based on a deep and sensitive understanding and respect for people of other faith traditions.

Her considerable knowledge of interfaith dialogue has been hammered out on the anvil of community experience. While others have been standing on the sidelines of interfaith encounter, shaking their heads and saying how difficult it all is, she has been getting on with the task and making a difference in real live situations both in the West Midlands and in South London.

I first met her when she worked in South London and I was Bishop of Southwark. She not only held my official licence for her interfaith work, done under the auspices of the South London Industrial Mission, but she also carried my complete confidence in the manner in which she fulfilled a distinctive and pioneering ministry of bridge-building.

As we move towards the new millennium the importance of interfaith dialogue increases. There are daily reminders of the multicultural, multireligious nature of our society, but as yet, there is no widespread understanding of how we may relate meaningfully to people of other faiths.

It is not that people of faith and good will are reluctant to relate to each other, it is more often a case of not feeling competent to do so. We don't know enough about the other person's faith tradition and we are uncertain how to approach them. We are afraid, perhaps, that we might unintentionally offend by the things we may do or say.

Friends on the Way will be of enormous help to us in this matter. Here is practical wisdom to ease our natural fear of relating to those who are of a different faith tradition. Here, in one story after another, is a rich vein of encounter and discovery that will cast an encouraging light on the challenge of interfaith co-operation within the local community.

Throughout Maureen Henderson's interfaith ministry she has humbly but firmly maintained her Christian conviction and tradition. But she has had the courage to explore encounters with those of other faiths and she has had the confidence to face the questions such encounters have raised.

As a result, her own faith and person has been enriched and we, and the whole church, have been placed in her debt.

† Roy Williamson

Formerly Bishop of Bradford
and Bishop of Southwark

I

Awakening

'What will you have to drink, Sister?'

I was hot, uncomfortable and embarrassed, sitting in the smoke filled public bar of the Walsall Town Hall, sipping orange juice along with two other sisters, Vivien and Gill. We were at a very crowded and tense political meeting, a far cry from the peace of the convent. What on earth were we doing there? Would the rest of the community approve? Was this really what sisters should be doing? Wouldn't we better at home, getting on with our prayers?

All these questions raced through my mind as we waited for the meeting to begin, and I was in fact very busy getting on with my prayers, just there. The atmosphere in Walsall in the summer of 1981 was very volatile. The rising rate of unemployment was aggravating racial tension, there had been a series of incidents and a proposed National Front march was liable to provoke more tension. The purpose of this meeting was to call for the march to be banned.

I am a member of an Anglican religious community dedicated to the Sacred Passion. Our full title is the Community of the Mission Sisters of the Sacred Passion of Jesus. We were founded on Zanzibar Island by Bishop Frank Weston in 1911 for prayer and missionary work in Africa. Since that time the sisters have been involved in teaching, nursing, pastoral work and evangelism, and I had worked for ten years as a nurse in Tanzania. For a variety of reasons, towards the end of the 1970s, we realized that our work in Africa was coming to an end. We felt that with our African experience we could make a contribution in multi-racial Britain. Several sisters returned to England at the end of

the 1970s and the early 1980s and about that time we received
an invitation from a group of parishes in Walsall to be part of
their life in South Walsall. The plan was for the local churches
and a housing trust to build a complex of sheltered accommodation, a day centre for the elderly and disabled and a convent
for the sisters who would be the night wardens. The aim was to
have six sisters as a praying presence.

At the time we responded to this invitation, the plans were
only on paper and we were offered a council house as temporary
accommodation. This idea produced varied responses. Some of
the sisters were delighted, others willing to give it a try. Some
parishioners were horrified. 'You can't put the sisters in Talke
Road!' This was a fine example of the power of the stereotype.
We were in fact very happy in Talke Road and it radically
influenced the direction in which our ministry developed.

Three sisters were chosen to start the venture and my companions were to be Vivien and Gillian Mary, the latter usually
known as Gill. Vivien, aged seventy-five, a retired teacher and
headmistress, was at that time away nursing her sister, so Gill
and I prepared for the great venture. We were both nurses and
had worked together in Tanzania. We had spent most of our
working lives living and working in institutions and were to find
ourselves very vulnerable and exposed in our new surroundings.
The main convent was at East Hanningfield in Essex at that time
and we loaded up the community car with what we hoped
would be adequate resources. We were used to working in
hospitals and coming off duty to meals already prepared. Now
it was to be a DIY life. 'We'll live on bread and cheese,' we said
cheerfully. 'You won't be able to afford it,' said the housekeeping sister grimly.

We were driven to Walsall, accompanied by the Sister
Superior, at the end of December 1980. It was a grey, overcast
day, typical of so many days we were to experience in the West
Midlands. I think Gill and I both felt a mixture of excitement
and apprehension, wondering what we were in for. Walsall is a
town of great contrasts: one moment you are in a leafy suburb
and the next in a run-down area. At that time of the year the

council estate looked quite grim and did not lift our fearful spirits. As soon as the car drew up outside the house we were surrounded by the local children, anxious for a diversion in their school holidays and fascinated by the prospect of nuns as neighbours. We were to discover later that they weren't the only ones to be fascinated. Many of their questions reflected adults' conversation at home. 'What made you leave your nunnery?' 'It's very unusual for nuns to live in a council house!'

The children helped us unpack the car and carry suitcases and boxes into the house. Their welcome completely transformed our impression of the area. Such willing hands soon completed the task, although not without some anxiety as Michael, aged eight, picked up a box nearly as big as himself. His brother came to the rescue and between them there was nearly a disaster, for, not anticipating such ready help, we had not labelled all the fragile boxes.

We entered a house made into a welcoming home all ready for us. We had seen it some months earlier and the transformation was astounding. The house had been decorated by a local Youth Opportunity Programme scheme and local parishioners had furnished the house completely. The kitchen contained gas cooker and washing machine but wasn't fully equipped with utensils as it was thought better that we should choose our own. With our limited experience of housekeeping we did not discover what we needed until we began to test out our culinary skills, when, reaching for the necessary, we discovered that it was not there. Comfortable chairs, cheerful curtains and cushions all contributed to a welcoming home. A bowl of fruit, a dish of sweets and a hot pot in the oven ready for lunch completed the welcome, and we readily abandoned our cheese sandwiches. At least we would get one good meal before we started fending for ourselves. The children left us to unpack and we went upstairs to explore further. The house had four bedrooms, one of which had been converted into a chapel. The other bedrooms had been prepared for us and the beds made up. I was delighted to find my room with bright, blue curtains and bedspread to match. It was very different from convent furnishings. Thinking it to be the proper thing, I had asked for regulation bedspreads before leaving the convent (they look like palls, being blue with a very large red cross). 'Be content with what you are given in Walsall,' I was told. No problem. I was very content with the new look!

The welcome of that house was quite overwhelming. It was as if the fairies had done it, as those responsible had left us alone to unpack and settle in. Not so the children. As soon as we had finished lunch and said goodbye to the car and those who had brought us from East Hanningfield, there was a bang on the front door. The children had returned. 'We've come to visit ya!' There began a steady stream of visitors as the news spread and groups of children arrived on the doorstep. We received them in small groups and were bombarded with questions. 'What time do you go to bed?' 'Do you wear that thing in bed?' pointing to the veil. 'What time do you get up?' More revealingly, 'Why do you have a room each?'

Eventually, worn out by this neighbourliness, we had to say, 'No more visitors today please, because we want to pray.' 'We want to pray with you,' came the enthusiastic reply. So upstairs we went to the chapel, where we had many more questions and a few prayers.

That first day set the trend for our ministry. We quickly established our community pattern of daily eucharist, five-fold Daily Office, personal prayer and silence. We shared the household chores, gardening and shopping and found that the latter gave us opportunities for many friendships and insights into local culture. 'This is the shop that robs ya!' said one of the children pointing to a local corner shop. 'I see it's your turn to get the dinner, Sister' said a neighbour as one of us queued at the local fish and chip shop.

We had no car and trailed to the shops with a shopping trolley. Very easy to fill up at the supermarket but a very different story when trying to get it on the bus. We soon discovered what a favoured and protected life we had so far had. We were in an ordinary council house, very accessible to the neighbours and soon became a source for change for the meter and the borrowing of tea, sugar and household utensils. It all gave us a ready access to the news and local issues of the neighbourhood.

Although we had been told that we were being invited for our praying presence, not our work, inevitably there were expectations as to what the sisters would do and some people were to be rather disappointed. We asked the parishes to allow us three months to get to know the local area and people before undertaking any long-term work. Our good relationship with the children, as well as being a source of fun and rapid learning of the local culture, stood us in good stead in building good relationships with our neighbours. The neighbourhood was to be transformed when spring came, with some gardens full of flowers and the occasional cherry tree. Even the gardens that grew dandelions were cheerful in the spring although a bane to gardeners. 'I don't know why you bother,' said Vivien one day after I had spent an industrious hour digging the dandelions out of the lawn. Pointing next door, she drew my attention to the finest set of dandelion clocks you could imagine.

We were all keen gardeners and as the council estate was built in the 1930s we had good long gardens. The previous occupants had looked after the back garden so we did not have a difficult task. We managed to grow a cheerful assortment of flowers and some of our own vegetables. One year we had a bumper crop of runner beans and begged friends to help themselves. It was beginner's luck. In other years we discovered that the short season of warm weather one often gets in the Midlands is not good for runner beans. Late frosts delayed them starting and one year an early frost took them just as they were cropping well. We got a lot of offers of help from the children who loved the job of watering, which we soon discovered could be overdone, especially where gro-bags were concerned. As Vivien wryly said one day in her typically direct manner, 'One child is some help, two is none!'

The front garden was more problematic. Our predecessors had pulled down the front wall and dug out a car port which was just a big hole. The people decorating our house had filled up the hole with all the rubbish left in the house and covered it with a (not very deep) layer of earth. That first winter was pretty wet and, by the time spring came, our front garden was sprouting bedsprings and bits of carpet. The men from the council came and rebuilt the wall but we were left with this unpleasant eyesore.

Vivien, ever resourceful, found a solution. A Neighbourhood Office was being built nearby and Vivien noticed the heap of rubble being cleared away. Getting into conversation with the men working on the site, she asked them what they were going to do with this rubble. 'We take it to the tip, Sister.' 'Well, our front garden is only round the corner. Would you like to dump it there?'

The first thing Gill and I knew about this was the arrival of a heap of rubble in the street outside our house. 'What ever do you think you are doing? Who do you think is going to move that lot? We shall get had for obstructing the highway!' A quick phone call to our friends on the Community Programme. 'We'll be round in the morning, Sister.'

Next day a group of lads arrived, none too thrilled with the job in prospect. Their supervisor left them, confident of their being well-occupied for the rest of the morning. Not to be out done in resourcefulness, they managed to get help from the scrap merchants who lived opposite and a JCB digger accomplished the task in a very short time. So the lads had a restful morning sitting on the front wall smoking until the supervisor returned.

It still didn't look very pretty but the same employment team was working on a church extension in another part of Walsall. This meant that topsoil and turf would soon be available and within weeks Vivien, helped by some of the local children, had laid a reasonably flat lawn which the children then thought they had every right to play on.

The story of council house repairs or lack of them is legendary. We had two main complaints. One was a piece of guttering that did not allow proper drainage. The water overflowed so that we had an almost permanent wet path and a dangerous hazard in icy weather. We lost count of the local councillors we had round to inspect it; we tried every colour and hue. Eventually when the local Neighbourhood Office was opened, the neighbourhood officer arranged for the job to be done for us.

A problem which was never dealt with while we were in residence was the fence at the bottom of the garden. Beyond the fence was a sort of no-man's land where rubbish had been dumped for years. There was an amazing assortment of bedsteads, carpets, mattresses and broken unknowns. The garden fence was sagging inwards with the weight of this eyesore and we visualized the imminent collapse of the fence and subsequent invasion of the garden and the flattening of our runner beans. Every time there was an election and politicians arrived canvassing on the doorstep, whether local or national, we had a solemn procession down the garden, usually led by Vivien, to view this 'unpleasance'. Nothing was done and the fence did not in fact collapse until after we had moved to our new convent.

One evening after a political meeting in town we were given a lift by someone who did not know our situation. He had been asked by some of our friends to bring us home as it was late at night and they were concerned for the safety of the sisters. As he drove up Talke Road and approached the house he gasped and said, 'Hey. This is not convent territory!'

We were certainly in very different surroundings from our former convent life. There was sufficient that was familiar in our pattern of life to give us stability. Our regular pattern of prayer was the framework in which all our other activities took place. It gave us the vision and the energy to keep exploring, as we sought to discover the mission God was calling us to in Walsall. As we were founding a new house, the Reverend Mother had given us some freedom to experiment with certain aspects of our rule of life in order to discover a lifestyle that was appropriate for our ministry. When we first arrived we decided we did not want silent meals or the lesser silence during the day. The lesser silence meant that for most of the morning and afternoon we only spoke about necessary work. At first we experienced a sense of freedom, but as life became more demanding we found we had lost something and were becoming very tired. We were living in very close proximity to each other and little things were beginning to grate. We desperately needed to give each other space. So we found ourselves taking back the rules of silence in order to do just that. At the end of a busy morning we welcomed a silent meal as very restful and a time for reflection although we enjoyed a chat over a cuppa after the washing up was done. There was a real sense in which certain customs and rules acquired the dimension of a gift for greater freedom, rather than an external imposition to restrict our freedom.

As we settled into life on the council estate we came to see the value of living our life in as open a way as possible so that people could drop in for a cup of tea and chat or join in one of our prayer times. We were very accessible in a house just like all the others and I always enjoyed the amazement of salesmen who called when I opened the door dressed in the traditional habit. I well remember the embarrassment of a young man selling leisure magazines with his thumb over the picture of one he obviously thought unsuitable for my viewing.

Learning to find our way in this very new environment was leading us to see that mission is about very everyday, earthy things which affect people's quality of life. It is about a good environment, safe streets, house repairs, drains and disposal of refuse. It is about good neighbours, children's activities, friendship, respect and good communication, bridging the generation gap, about a sense of solidarity and belonging, of taking responsibility for our neighbourhood. God's mission is about human flourishing and he invites us all to share in his work of bringing fullness of life to all.

2

We Can't Do It Alone

Life is about relationships and we were discovering just how important these were. Our friendship with the children was so important. Neighbours who might be shy of approaching us would often do it through the children. A street party was planned in July 1981 to celebrate the Royal Wedding. The children from across the road came with a request from their mother who was organizing the party. If she provided the ingredients would we make the cakes? I am not sure why it is assumed that sisters will be good at making cakes. We did not feel able to take on all the cooking but we readily agreed to make a contribution. The day turned out to be gloriously sunny and the party was a great success and further cemented neighbourhood relations. We were not so thrilled with the disco that followed that night. We were directly opposite the music system and the volume was unbelievable. The curate of the parish found two shattered sisters on his doorstep as Vivien and Gill fled from the noise. I was paralysed by a headache by that time and could only go to bed. As my bedroom was in the front of the house, in direct line of the sound, I could only abandon myself to the agony. The next thing I knew was waking up at 3 am to a deathly hush. I couldn't believe that I had slept through it.

Two ladies, who were friends of our community, wrote to say that they would like to pay us a visit. As they were used to visiting our main convent we wondered what they would make of our situation, but we dutifully invited them to afternoon tea. We managed to entertain them for two hours but there was a feeling that we were not quite on the same wave length.

Eventually the time came for them to depart, only to discover that they had left their lights on and the battery was flat. Vivien and I looked at each other in horror, our silence spoke volumes as we contemplated having to entertain them for another few hours.

'What's your problem, Sister?' called one of the children passing. On learning our predicament, they said, 'No problem,' and within minutes a crowd descended upon us with jump leads and the JCB digger. The crowd was a splendid collection of local culture with the mother of the family opposite in charge. She was dressed for action, arms covered with tattoos, and obviously a force to be reckoned with. Our visitors looked more than a little alarmed, but soon the car was running and they drove off, maybe a little dazed after their adventure. We were left, feeling at last truly part of the local community. We had been the source of support, advice, small change, household goods and now we were on the receiving end. There was a great deal of mutual satisfaction as we expressed our thanks. 'A pleasure, Sisters, any time,' and we knew that to be true.

One incident which showed the value of united action occurred when our windows were changed. Suddenly, unannounced, workers arrived mid-December to change the window frames. The old windows were taken out and the new ones inserted at the end of one week. I was fortunate to go away that weekend. It snowed hard and I returned to find Vivien and Gill living in arctic conditions with gaping holes stuffed with newspaper. They were literally blue with cold, although their fury helped generate some heat. Fortunately, the plasterers arrived shortly after to fill up the gaps. However, the debris from the old windows was just left on the front lawn. (Our beautiful lawn tended so lovingly by Vivien.) Anything remotely useful disappeared fairly quickly, but the rubbish lay there for months.

We complained to the neighbourhood officer and then the councillors, all to no avail. Eventually, tired of living in such depressing surroundings and very angry at the way the well-being of the neighbourhood was being ignored, we said we would pay no more rent until the rubbish was removed. The news of an impending rent strike led by the sisters had a dramatic effect and the very next day a lorry arrived to remove not only our rubbish, but that of our neighbours too.

Through all this activity we maintained our life of prayer and we, together with those who came to share some of our prayer times, found our chapel an oasis of peace. The passing transistor radios or ice-cream vans only served to deepen that peace when they had passed, although the repetitive thud of a football in the road did get us down sometimes. The children played in the street often until very late at night on summer evenings. Winter did have the advantage of giving us more sleep. One day, Vivien came in laughing. 'They are playing musical bits of paper. Tracy is singing and when she stops they all jump on a piece of paper.' Knowing the usually inexhaustible supply of sweet and chip papers in the street, I asked if anyone was ever out!

Traditionally, Passion Sunday, the fifth Sunday in Lent, has been a day when the community has kept a twenty-four hour vigil of prayer and silence at the Mother House. We decided to have a twelve-hour vigil and invite friends and members of the local churches to join us for half-hour periods. This event has become a regular part of our life in Walsall, but that first year in the council house was very special. We had a quiet morning and then after lunch a steady stream of people came; sometimes the chapel was so full that there was no room for a sister.

Late afternoon we suddenly heard the familiar voice of Christopher, aged ten, reading the notice on our front door. 'Please do not knock, just push the door open and come in. The chapel is upstairs.' Bump went the door and a group of children appeared at the foot of the stairs. 'Ssh,' I warned, putting my finger over my lips. 'We are praying.' 'We want to pray too.' So as quietly as possible we went upstairs and fortunately at that time only Vivien was in the chapel. The children all left quite soon after a quick look round, but Michael, aged eight, stayed kneeling, obviously fascinated. 'Say a prayer, Sister,' he whispered. I was so overcome by the wonder of the moment that all

I could say was, 'Dear God, thank you for Michael.' After a short silence and a hug, Michael left very quietly. I shall never forget that moment. Prayer is just being there.

The three parishes which had invited us to Walsall covered the areas of Fullbrook, Palfrey and Caldmore. The populations of Palfrey and Caldmore were very multiracial with large Asian and Afro-Caribbean communities. We lived in Fullbrook, in St Gabriel's parish, and were also involved in the worship and activities of St Michael's, Caldmore and St Mary's, Palfrey. The Revd Peter Barnett, priest in charge at St Michael's Church, was very involved in the local community and so introduced the sisters to a wide variety of people. He led us on a very intensive 'induction course' when we first arrived in Walsall. It was a case of 'in at the deep end'. I will always be grateful to Peter for his vision and energy, although it was often hard to keep pace with him. He was part of an ecumenical network, later to be formalized into a local Covenant for Unity scheme. There were Roman Catholic, Methodist, United Reformed and Baptist churches in Caldmore and ecumenical relationships were real and very active.

The Revd Frank Amery, from Caldmore Methodist Church, was on our doorstep to welcome us on the day after our arrival in Walsall. Frank was a great support and help to the sisters in those early days. His quiet and gentle manner covered a very deep wisdom and inspirational leadership and we learnt much from him. Later developments in our ministry built on the solid foundations he, and others like Peter Barnett, had helped to lay in good community relations. There were large Sikh and Muslim populations in the locality and the first purpose built Sikh Temple or Gurdwara was in Caldmore. Rutter Street Mosque was opposite Caldmore Methodist Church and there were very cordial relations between the members of the Mosque and the Methodist Church.

Frank tells how the first contact came when the members of the Mosque were planning their new building. At that time the Muslim community was meeting in a house which was far too small for the community and had no heating. There was a problem over car parking as the Local Authority stipulated that the Mosque must provide one car space for every four places for people in the Mosque. The Imam and some leaders in the Muslim community approached Frank to see if they could share car parking space. The Methodist Church had a reasonably sized car park which church members were not going to be using at the same time as the Muslims. So a workable way of sharing car parking was agreed. There was a school room behind the church which was let out to the local community and the Muslims were allowed to rent it for weddings, receptions and other social occasions.

One of the very formative influences, in our transition from traditional convent life and missionary work to this new life, was the existence of the Walsall Council of Churches. This was a very active ecumenical organization, not only in arranging joint worship and study but practical service and witness to the people of Walsall. The Community Exchange programme was an important sub group. COMEX, as it was called, was responsible for a community centre and a large scheme for the unemployed, run in those days under the Manpower Services Commission. In the early days this work was run from the Glebe Centre in Caldmore, a Community and Worship Centre built by the United Reformed Church. The Glebe Centre provided a drop-in centre for the unemployed and also provided training and work placements. Later the provision of schemes for the unemployed developed and became a very large organization occupying several sites in Walsall.

The sisters became involved with this work and regularly attended the Friday prayer and reflection group at St Michael's Church, Caldmore which was followed by lunch. This was a valuable place for support and growing understanding of the needs and issues around. The diversity in the group was wonderful. We had the clergy from the local churches but also painters, carpenters, builders and electricians with no theological training who, when the clergy allowed them to get a word in, challenged us all by their wisdom and insight. Here was a real working theology and we discovered the value of this dialogue, although

it was not without its moments of conflict and misunderstanding.

There was an ecumenical fraternal consisting of the clergy
in Caldmore together with COMEX volunteers and other interested lay people. The sisters were invited to join this group
which met fortnightly in one anothers' houses. Those hosting
the group provided tea and a topic for discussion and prayer.
We met at 5.30 pm and usually continued until 7 pm when
people had to leave for their evening meetings. This sharing of
concerns, problems and ideas was a great source of strength for
the sisters in the often confusing and overwhelming early days
when we were bombarded with new experiences. So much
seemed light years away from our traditional convent life and
we could easily have become overloaded. We listened and learnt
much from people who had a great deal of experience and were
in turn delighted and humbled to realize that we were valued for
who we were as well as our life of prayer.

Our association with the Caldmore ecumenical network and
COMEX was a very significant experience. There was a rich
combination of spiritual fellowship provided by the fraternal,
the Friday lunchtime meetings and occasional quiet days, and
the working together on a variety of practical projects.

I was a member of the COMEX management committee and
helped with the community centre. The issue of unemployment,
particularly for the young, was a major concern for us and
when the 1981 March for Jobs came through Walsall, the
sisters felt bound to join in. This was a very new venture for us
and involved considerable prayer and heart searching before we
took the decision to march. We had never done such a thing
before; we did not get involved in politics and we were aware
that we would incur considerable disapproval from some
quarters. However, we were so involved with working with the
unemployed that we felt our credibility would be in question if
we held back. We could not endorse all that was said by our
fellow marchers but we were quite clear about our stand regarding the evils of mass unemployment and were prepared to risk
censure and misunderstanding. It was made easier for us by the

strong stand which the then Bishop of Lichfield (the Rt Revd Kenneth Skelton) took in leading the procession when it passed through his diocese.

The sisters joined the marchers when they arrived at the Walsall borough boundary in Darlaston Road and marched into town, causing some consternation amongst those church members who disapproved of getting involved in politics. By this time we were convinced that doing nothing was also a political act since it was to support the present unsatisfactory and unjust situation. The marchers spent the night in St Michael's church hall in Caldmore and volunteers, including the sisters, got up early to provide breakfast the next morning. When the marchers set off again the sisters accompanied them as far as Wednesbury.

This event represented a watershed in the sisters' ministry. I well remember a man walking beside us, amazed at our presence. 'I can't get over you sisters walking with us. The church has done things *for* us but has never done things *with* us.'

That remark made a deep impression upon me. Doing things for others maintains a position of power; it is often done on our terms and may be of more benefit to us. Doing things with people involves risk, powerlessness, misunderstanding and possible failure but it is more likely to meet the needs of people where they are and continue after we have gone. It is about empowering people to change their own lives. I became quite convinced of the importance of being prepared to get our hands dirty, of rubbing shoulders with a variety of people whose views we might not always agree with, but who share a common concern to oppose those things which diminish people's humanity.

An example of the complications of working with such a variety of people is shown in our friendship with Brian. Brian was the leader of the local Trades Council and we met him while taking part in the March for Jobs. He seemed to feel that the sisters needed to be taken under his wing, particularly when we encountered some unpleasantness from some local National Front members. I had been quite outspoken in my opposition to them and it had been reported in the local press. One Sunday evening, on the way home from church, the sisters were surrounded by a gang of youths asking if we were the sisters against the National Front and when I challenged them, they informed us that they would 'do our house over'.

I did not take it very seriously but our friends did and Brian got to hear about it. The Sikh Gurdwara in Caldmore had been vandalized and the Sikh community was very nervous. A group of local people mounted guard over the Gurdwara at night for several weeks and Brian got them to drive past our house several times a night to see that we were all right. Brian was particularly anxious when Gill and I were going away for our Community Chapter and would be leaving Vivien alone. He turned up on the doorstep and offered to sleep in the sitting room to ensure her safety. 'Brian, I shall have other problems if you do,' was her response.

Some time later Brian arrived looking very pleased with himself. 'You've no need to worry any more. You will be quite safe. I've told the National Front that if anyone touches so much as a hair on one of the sisters' heads, something will happen to Charlie!' (the leader of the local branch). 'Brian,' I remonstrated in horror, 'you can't do that.' Brian wagged his finger at me. 'Sister, I don't interfere with the way you conduct your affairs. You leave me to do this my way.' No more was said and we were left in peace.

All this led up to the political meeting I mentioned at the beginning of chapter 1. Brian remained a good friend and kept us informed of local news and through him we got an invitation to the meeting at the Town Hall. There was a divergence of opinion with the Local Authority and the Police as to the best way to deal with the proposed National Front march. Some thought it better to let it go ahead and contain the activity, others that it would be far too inflammatory and provoke violence. In the end the march was banned.

It was in this unlikely setting that I received a clear sense of the next phase in my ministry. As I looked around at the turbans and skull caps I reflected that many of us were people of faith. This was what mattered most to many of us, gave us the motivation for our activity for social justice and it was on that level that we must meet. This was the moment when the idea of the Walsall Interfaith Group was born. This was to prove a huge shift in our understanding of a missionary vocation and we could only take things a step at a time. Looking back on those early days I can now see how, through the events and challenges of our daily life, the Spirit was providing those gentle but firm nudges in this direction.

3

Discovering More Neighbours

Vivien's friendship with the neighbourhood officer, our work and contacts with COMEX and the growing number of friends made while engaging with issues in the local community meant that we were working with a great variety of people who shared our concerns for a more just and peaceful society. We found that we did have values in common, although we might come to them from different perspectives. Through people like Brian we came to respect those other view points.

Our first major venture into the interfaith arena came as a result of racial incidents in the summer of 1981. Racist graffiti were daubed on the walls of the local Sikh Gurdwara and the Sikh community was very nervous. We had already made friends with some of the members through our political activities. We wanted them to know of our support and rather than just say 'we will pray for you', we decided to telephone one of our friends and ask if we could come and pray for peace with them at the Gurdwara. We had never visited such a place before and thought long and hard before making the suggestion. We were not at all sure that we could pray in the Gurdwara, yet there was this deep urge to do just that.

I was conscious of some nervousness both because it was such new territory and also because it was likely to produce censure from other Christians. How could we go into such places where they worship other gods? Were we not betraying the Christian faith? I was painfully aware of such questions. Yet I felt bound to respond to the vulnerability of those who were neighbours and fellow citizens. It was as if we were being pushed to do something which we would understand later.

It was arranged that we should attend evening prayers and on arrival we were met by our Sikh friends with exquisite courtesy. As we entered the building we were asked to remove our shoes and wash our hands before going upstairs into the Gurdwara. The word Gurdwara means gateway to the Guru. Sikhism came into being in the Punjab in the fifteenth and sixteenth centuries. There were ten Gurus during this time, the first being Guru Nanak. Guru Gobind Singh was the last living Guru who founded the Khalsa and decreed that the holy book compiled during these centuries should, after his death, be regarded as the living Guru. So the holy book, known as the Guru Granth Sahib, is the focal point of Sikh worship and is treated with the utmost respect.

On entering the prayer hall which was covered with lovely soft carpet we approached the platform which held the Guru Granth Sahib. We gave a little bow of our head to show our respect before taking our place with the Sikh women on the left side of the hall. Sikhs prostrate before the Guru Granth Sahib, but we felt that our bow was an appropriate expression of respect without compromising our beliefs. As we sat cross legged on the floor (quite difficult if you are not used to it), we were thankful for our long habits.

The service at the Gurdwara was all in Punjabi and we could not understand a single word, but we picked up the atmosphere. It was one of great reverence and devotion. We felt a deep sense of the holy. There was a sizable congregation which was impressive for a weekday. On Sundays there would be a much larger congregation and on festivals the place would be packed. The men sat on the right side of the prayer hall and the women and children on the left. There was a wonderful mixture of reverence and informality. The women were dressed in beautiful, brightly-coloured salwar suits and the children played quietly amongst them, only being restrained when they became too boisterous.

We all faced a brightly-coloured canopy covering a platform. Raised up on the platform, surrounded by exquisitely embroidered cloths, was the Holy Book, the Guru Granth Sahib. A priest or Granthi sat behind the Holy Book, gently waving a horse tail fly switch. In front were flowers and offerings from the people. To the right were singers playing harmonium and drums. The songs are usually taken from the Holy Book, which is full of hymns of praise. The Holy Book was compiled by the fifth Guru, Guru Arjan, who wrote many of the hymns. Works of both Muslim and Hindu holy men are also included.

The singing of hymns of praise with commentaries on them took up the main part of the worship, which was concluded by the Granthi reading from the Guru Granth Sahib and saying the final prayers. The Holy Book was then wrapped in beautiful cloths, placed on the head of the Granthi and carried in procession upstairs and ceremonially put to rest on a bed in a special room called the Sachkhand. The service ended with the distribution of Kraah Prashaad which is usually a mixture of semolina, sugar and ghee (clarified butter). A small amount is put into the hands of everyone present as a symbol that no one goes away from the Guru empty-handed or unblessed.

We found ourselves very able to pray in this place. There was a real sense of the presence of God and we prayed silently for these people and for peace for them and all the people of Walsall. When the service of worship was over, the secretary gave out the notices and welcomed the sisters, explaining why we had come. I was then invited to say a few words and was able to convey the concern of members of the local churches and assure the Sikh community of our continued prayers and support.

The congregation went downstairs but we stayed to be introduced to some of the members and were shown the distinctive parts of the Gurdwara. Around the walls were pictures showing important aspects of the story of Sikhism. On the walls near the canopy were the symbols of Sikhism and pictures of Guru Nanak and Guru Gobind Singh. There was also a large picture of the Golden Temple at Amritsar, a central focus and holy place for Sikhs, built by Guru Arjan. The history of Sikhism dates from the birth of Guru Nanak in 1469: and the tenth and last Guru, Guru Gobind Singh, died in battle in 1708.

During this period of just over two centuries the political

scene was very turbulent. Some of the Gurus were imprisoned
and tortured and Guru Arjan was roasted to death on a red hot
iron plate. The ninth Guru, Guru Tegh Bahadur, was publicly
beheaded as a result of his attempt to oppose the forcible con-
version of Hindus to Islam. Two of his companions were killed;
one was boiled in a cauldron of water, the other was sawn alive.
Pictures of this history were displayed on the walls of the
Gurdwara in very graphic detail and as we walked round the
Gurdwara, looking at the pictures and hearing the stories, I was
reminded of the devotion of the Stations of the Cross. Guru
Nanak had travelled extensively on preaching tours and a map
of this was displayed. Here I was reminded of maps of Paul's
missionary journeys and how important it is for a community to
remember and celebrate its history.

We then went downstairs for Langer, which is the shared
meal provided for all the worshippers. It is considered part of
the worship and was instigated by the third Guru, Guru Amar
Das as a way to overcome the restrictions of the caste system.
He decreed that a free kitchen service was to be attached to
every Sikh place of worship, so that people of all religions,
castes, colours or creeds could sit down together and lose all
ideas of untouchability and superiority of one people over
another.

Families take it in turns to provide and cook the food. It is
considered a great honour to do this and family anniversaries
are frequently celebrated by providing the free kitchen. If
you like spicy food this is a wonderful occasion. The food is
always vegetarian and no alcohol or tobacco is allowed on the
premises. We ate delicious vegetable curry and chapatis with
yoghurt, followed by milk pudding flavoured with nuts and
spices.

During this time we were able to ask questions and learn
about the distinctive symbols of Sikhism. We had already
become familiar with the presence of the Sikh community in
Walsall because of their turbans. We were amazed to learn that
the turban or 'Dastar' is five yards long. It is worn by the men
and boys as soon as they are able to manage the tying of the

long piece of cloth. Until then, young boys have their hair tied up and covered with a little cloth. The turban is worn to cover the long hair which is never cut according to devout Sikh custom. This expresses the belief that we should live as God created us and is known as 'Kesh'. A wooden comb or 'Kangha', necessary for keeping long hair clean and tidy, is another symbol.

Our attention was drawn to the iron bangle or 'Kara' which both the men and women were wearing on their right arm. This is a symbol of the brotherhood and sisterhood of the Khalsa. The men in full ceremonial dress wear the sword or 'Kirpan' as a symbol of a Sikh's independence and fearlessness. Most Sikhs present were wearing a small replica. The fifth symbol, we were told, was the 'Kachhehra' or shorts worn by the men symbolizing self restaint.

These five 'Kakaars' or 'Ks', symbols of the Khalsa or brotherhood of Sikhs, were given by the tenth Guru, Guru Gobind Singh, when he instituted the Khalsa. The bangle and the sword appear on the Sikh flag which is flown outside the Gurdwara.

We were struck by the wisdom and sincerity of these people and the pride with which they spoke of their history and religious practice. There was a deep sense of tranquility about them which came from a rootedness in both God and their tradition. This first visit gave me a sense of being on the edge of a very rich and exciting experience, a glimpse of a new perspective on life, an opening up of new dimensions.

After sharing the meal we took leave of our hosts and went home feeling greatly enriched by the experience. There was so much to ponder. We were left with the impression of having met true people of God. Many Sikhs will shake hands but a more traditional greeting is to put the hands together in an attitude of prayer and give a little bow, thereby acknowledging the divine presence in the other person. This really summed up the experience of our visit. We had indeed met God in these people. They had a very different story and approached God through different symbols, yet we found that we had so much in common. The atmosphere in the Gurdwara was so conducive to prayer and the hospitality we received very Christlike. We felt in no doubt that we were all on a similar journey in the search to be human and the search for God.

This visit was the first of many as we got to know each other better. Everyone was welcome at the Gurdwara any time and would always be given a drink and food. I soon learnt that in the course of developing the Walsall Interfaith Group, whenever I visited anyone, I must allow time for refreshments. It is considered very bad manners to rush into one's business without giving time for the courtesies. I found this very challenging to my busy lifestyle and it taught me to savour life and so enjoy more fully the people with whom I was working. I have come to see that enjoyment is so important. If we enjoy people we will accept and appreciate their uniqueness and be free from the desire to change them. We have so much to learn from each other and enjoyment can free us to receive the gifts God wants to give us through each other.

My friendship with members of other faith traditions during my time in Walsall was such an enrichment. We visited each other's homes and drank many cups of tea together. Our respect and affection for each other grew as we came to see how much we had in common. The differences became more interesting than threatening. One Muslim friend came to visit us and he was clearly mystified by our lifestyle and conversation was a little stilted. When we took him to see our chapel he asked what all the chairs were for and was surprised to hear that we sat for much of our worship. However, when we explained the pattern of the Daily Office and that we prayed five offices or formal prayer times, his face lit up. 'You pray five times daily. That is how we pray,' and the conversation began to flow as we discovered that we had this in common.

As we grew in friendship our shared humanity and concerns became more important than our differences. One notable example of this process concerned a member of our church congregation who lived opposite the Sikh Gurdwara. She was scandalized to see the sisters coming out of the Gurdwara one day and later plucked up courage to speak to us about it. 'How can you visit such a place? They worship false gods.' Our re-assurances did little to allay her fears and we had to agree to differ.

Some months later she told us how she was becoming friendly with her Sikh neighbours. It all started when a little girl, Sukhjit, was preparing for a cookery lesson and needed to weigh ingredients ready to take to school. Her mother had no kitchen scales, never having needed them with her traditional cooking. Sukhjit shyly came to ask if she could use Mrs B's scales. Mrs B responded warmly and through this incident became friendly with her parents. She was often greeted by another family living nearby when passing their house and one day she was invited in for a cup of tea. The Sikh family was wonderfully supportive when Mrs B's husband died and very concerned that she was living alone. Mrs B was more or less adopted as an aunt to their daughter Mandy and they all became very fond of each other. Through this human encounter Mrs B's attitude to Sikhs radically changed. They began to invite each other to celebrate family festivals, Mandy's birthday being the first one. Mrs B was invited to look round the Gurdwara and invited to several weddings. She was heart-broken when the family later moved to Canada. The following year I heard that she had been invited to have a holiday with them in Canada which she thoroughly enjoyed and subsequently the experience has been repeated.

Through all these encounters we discovered that the most important thing about us is that we are human and that our faith traditions are particular ways of being human. When we met each other as neighbours and shared common concerns we found that our shared joys and sorrows overrode our differ-ences in belief. In supporting each other in times of difficulty and celebrating our joys together we learnt so much about each other's customs and the reasons for them. As the friendship deepened, so we came to accept and then value our differences. Those differences become marks of people for whom we had a growing affection and respect and we didn't want to change them. The enjoyment of friendship was a liberating thing because we ceased to want to change people and make them like us.

4

How Did I Get Here?

I came from a family that was not particularly religious. My father was Irish and had been brought up as a Methodist. His mother had died in an influenza epidemic in 1914 leaving six children. Dad was the eldest at fourteen, the youngest being six months old. On him fell the burden of caring for his three brothers and two sisters. The boys did not get on with their father and all left home as soon as they could and most lost contact with each other. Dad joined the army and served in Palestine and then India. He was a great admirer of Gandhi and I remember the shock to him when Gandhi was assassinated. Although he professed to being an atheist, my impressions were that he was more anti-church than disbelieving in God. He had seen the stance the established church had taken both in Palestine and India and believed it to be contrary to the teachings of Jesus Christ, for whom he had a great admiration.

My mother came from the West Country and loved to tell people that she was born in a workhouse (her parents were master and matron of such an establishment in Calne). She was brought up as an Anglican, became a nurse and met my father while she was nursing at Kingston upon Thames. Mum went to work at the Royal Mineral Water Hospital in Bath. Dad followed her and they married at the beginning of 1938.

Dad did not want us to be baptized when we were children as he said that he did not want us to be 'brainwashed', rather we were to be free to make up our own minds when we became adults. My younger sister, Yvonne, died of meningitis when I was four years old and one of the things which increased my mother's grief was that Yvonne had died unbaptized. So when my second sister, Veronica, was born two years later, Mum put her foot down and Veronica and I were baptized together on 1 October 1944. It is one of my most vivid childhood memories and made a deep impression on me. Obviously my Godparents made the promises for me, but at that moment of standing on a chair beside the font at the back of the Church of St John the Evangelist, Lower Weston, Bath, I had a deep sense of something special happening to me.

I shall always be grateful for my father's stance since I was left free to search and question for myself. The next big religious moment was when I was eight. We shared a house with a Mr and Mrs Sargeant who ran a market garden. They were wonderfully kind to us and we never went short of good food during the war. Vegetables fresh from the garden the morning they were cooked tasted like nothing I have had since. Auntie Sargeant, as I called her, died in her sleep one night and when my mother came and sat on my bed to tell me in the morning my one question was, 'Where do people go when they die? What happens to them?' 'Nowhere,' said my mother. 'There is nothing.'

I remember looking out of the window at the sky and wondering what nothing was like. I just could not imagine it but that moment left its mark upon me.

There was one absolute rule my father insisted upon. On Sunday afternoon it was 'in bed or out of barracks!' Nothing was to disturb his Sunday afternoon sleep and so I was sent to Sunday school although I remember little about it. I do remember hearing the Easter story when I was about eight and being so upset that Jesus got killed. 'A lovely man like that and they killed him!' I was in tears. 'It's all right,' said a friend. 'He rises from the dead.' 'Don't be stupid,' I retorted, 'people don't rise from the dead.'

My father loved a good argument and religion and politics were his favourite topics. In my early teens I overheard a friend of the family arguing with my father. My father was saying that Christianity was too soft and easy. It was for women and people not quite right in the head. I remember the friend saying very quietly, 'Christ died for us. Was that easy?'

I had not been listening to the conversation and had my head buried in a book, but those words shot out at me. It was the conviction in that friend's voice which stunned me. I got up and went to my room in a state of shock. Did God really exist? Was that story about Jesus true after all? I was in a state of absolute confusion and I knelt down and tried to pray. I had little idea of how to go about it. It was just, 'God, if you are, show me.'

I began to take a bit more notice of school assembly. Some of my friends were preparing for confirmation, and I plucked up courage to ask my mother if I could be confirmed. Her response was, 'Oh, I suppose it's time you were done.' Those confirmation classes were very important to me. I am not sure how much I understood but I did want to know God and after confirmation the eight o'clock Holy Communion service, which I attended monthly, was a very important part of my life.

I grew up close to the earth. My parents were keen gardeners and we always had magnificent flower beds and a wonderful supply of fresh vegetables. The seasons were such an important part of life and became associated with certain varieties of flowers, fruit and vegetables. The first hard frost in the autumn, which left the dahlias limp and black, marked an important transition period. We lived on the outskirts of Bath and the fields were very close. There was a paddock next door where grass was grown for hay and one of my favourite flowers, moon daisies, were always tantalizingly out of reach in the mowing grass in which I was forbidden to walk. The hay making day was always a family and neighbour affair, with a picnic and homemade cider. From an early age I loved to walk alone across the fields and as I grew older so the walks got longer. Then I acquired a bicycle and my explorations increased. I was not sure how to relate to the God of Sunday school and church but I had a natural sense of a Presence in creation. I was not alone and I had a deep sense of belonging to the earth.

During my last year at school I was still unsure of my career. I had some vague idea of taking up horticulture but my parents did not seem keen and said that they could not afford to send me to college. In a fit of pique I said I was going to join the Wrens, which worried them even more. Then some one at church invited me along to a meeting of the Church Missionary Society. I reluctantly went along with my friend Jeanette, not at all sure what to expect. There was a film on medical work in Nigeria and I was appalled by the number of diseases which ruined the health of so many people. My imagination was particularly captured by the sight of people walking barefoot and contracting hookworm. I knew then that I was to train as a nurse and go to Africa to do something about it. I experienced a sense of light and my whole body being energized as the realization came. I remember nothing about the rest of the evening except a desire to be alone and a niggling worry about how I was going to tell my parents.

When I walked home with Jeanette after a Girl Guide meeting a few days later she said, 'Something happened to you the other night. What was it?' When I tentatively told her, she became very excited and wanted to tell everyone. I was not really ready for that but it did make me start taking some action. Without Jeanette's encouragement I might have just drifted. The next morning as I was putting on my school beret ready to leave the house I said, 'Mum, I want to train as a nurse and become a missionary in Africa.' End of speech and out of the door!

When I returned from school my mother was waiting for me. 'Do you really want to be a nurse? If so I will make an appointment at the hospital for you to see the Matron.' I was terrified, but I wasn't going to show it. I didn't even like hospitals. They smelt of disinfectant and I hated the sight of blood. How ever was I going to cope?

At the beginning of September I reported for duty at the Forbes Fraser Hospital as a pre-nursing student, as at seventeen I was too young to begin my general training. For my first week I went around in a daze, hating every minute of it and terrified of doing something wrong. I was introduced to bedpans and bed baths. I began to enjoy making people more comfortable and having conversations with very interesting people. I remember vividly at the end of the first week, standing on the balcony after making someone's bed and thinking, 'Yes, this is me. I have made the right choice after all.'

It was a moment of such affirmation and happiness and from then on I did not look back. However difficult things could be at times, I loved being a nurse.

One year I went to Lee Abbey, near Lynton in North Devon, for a week. It was a most wonderful holiday in beautiful surroundings. It provided everything I loved: beautiful country-side and the sea, long walks with a cream tea en route, and companionship with others who were searching for God. I was a little worried by the certainty of some people and there seemed to be a tendency by some to pressurize people into owning a particular kind of experience. But on the whole it was gentle and I lapped up the teaching on prayer and Bible study. Being with people for whom God was real made a deep impression upon me and the worship was like nothing I had experienced before. I was moved by the enthusiasm and combination of reverence and spontaneity.

I had several holidays at Lee Abbey and the person who influenced me most was the Revd Jack Winslow. The chaplaincy team included clergy of the different traditions within the Anglican Church and Jack was of the Catholic tradition. He had spent years in India as a missionary and had founded an Ashram at Poona. Jack was a man of prayer and his teaching on the 'Morning Watch', as he called it, started a life-long practice for me. He taught prayer as a relationship with God and he lived what he taught. I am very grateful for the time spent with Jack and I realize now that he sowed many seeds of things I did not understand at the time.

I completed my general training and went to London and Ipswich for midwifery training. Then I was ready to offer myself to the missionary society. But I wasn't; I was having a crisis of faith. I had spent some time with the Baptist Church as I found the Anglican Church so dull. But I could not accept the literalist interpretation of the Bible. Although I had allowed myself to be pushed into a particular practice, my whole being was not in it and I reacted and abandoned everything for a while. I was both disillusioned and confused and I thought I would give it all up. It was a terrible wilderness experience as I tried to live without God. I was also unhappy at work and so I decided to take a break.

I joined the Lee Abbey Community for a year, a strange place to go when you are trying to give up God! Here was a place where I felt at home, where I could explore and get help if needed. I arrived a bit cynical and definitely rebellious but they accepted me. The beauty of the place, the regular prayer life and companionship of such a diversity of people encouraged me to explore my own experience. Through the influence of the parish church in Lynton I became drawn to the Anglo-Catholic tradition. When the vicar celebrated the Sunday eucharist he was so wrapped in worship that I was drawn into that worship. Mystery and a sense of the holy drew me into adoration and an experience of worship which absorbed my whole being.

On leaving Lee Abbey I spent some time as a midwife and offered to the Society for the Propagation of the Gospel. In September 1964 I arrived at Bonda Hospital, Zimbabwe, where I worked for three and a half years as a ward sister and sister tutor. During this time I had a growing sense of being called to join a religious order. I loved to walk miles in the bush and climb the many kopjes in the Eastern Highlands, often alone or with Dorothy Marshall, a Mother's Union worker. I remember struggling with this sense of call as I gazed at the mountains. How could I give up my freedom?

Dorothy sensed my struggle and challenged me one day that I was thinking of joining a religious order. 'Yes,' I said. 'I am afraid that God is calling me to that.' 'Afraid,' she said. 'Why are you afraid? If you don't want it, don't do it.' It wasn't as simple as that. There was that niggle in the back of my mind which just would not go away. Eventually I got round to praying about it. 'God, I'll do it if you want me to, but you will have to show me which community because I'm not looking!' God gave me ten days. In the course of a conversation with Barbara

Wilden, with whom I shared a house, I confided my feelings.
'The only community I would consider joining is the Community of the Sacred Passion,' and she produced a brochure.
I only had to read the introduction about a life of prayer and missionary work in Africa and I knew that was it. Then I remembered my prayer of ten days earlier and, with a deep sense of awe, I said yes to God.

I returned to England in 1968 and after three months leave I went to the English house at East Hanningfield. There I spent eighteen months as a postulant and novice before going to Tanzania in December 1969. At the Mother House at Msalabani (place of the Cross in Swahili) Magila, I completed the further two years of the Novitiate and made my first profession on 14 February 1972. The service took place in the parish church, as a few days before my profession retreat, a high wind blew off a large part of the convent and chapel roof. When I related this news in a letter to my parents my father's reply was, 'God doesn't like what you are doing!'

My first profession of my desire to live under the vows of poverty, chastity and obedience was for one year, to be renewed annually for at least three years or until both I and my sisters thought I was ready to make life vows. Although living under temporary or simple vows, my intention was to be for a life-long commitment, beautifully expressed by the declaration made before the formal, legal words of profession.

'I desire to consecrate myself to God, body, soul and spirit; freely, wholly, devotedly;
to love, serve and glorify God in poverty, chastity and obedience.'

Those words I still use in my personal prayer at moments when I want to renew my commitment to God. I eventually made my solemn profession to life vows on 12 December 1975. I continued to work as a nurse and midwife until I returned to England in 1979 to take up new work and eventually ended up in Walsall.

When I arrived in Walsall I knew little about the world's other great religious traditions. Although I had spent ten years working alongside Muslims in Tanzania, I had learnt little about them apart from the observance of Ramadan. I took it for granted that Christianity was 'The Truth' and that other traditions, although containing some truth, were incomplete. I had not considered whether they were worshipping the same God, but I did assume that Christians had an intimate, personal relationship with God through Jesus which was not possible elsewhere. How those assumptions were to be challenged by the Walsall years!

5

The Walsall Interfaith Group

Our growing friendship with such a diversity of people in Walsall meant that we cared deeply about what happened to one another and were increasingly wanting to work together to improve the quality of life for our respective communities. After the events of summer 1981, with the mounting racial tension and National Front activity, I became convinced that we should be moving towards greater co-operation between people of the different faith traditions in Walsall. There was already a good network of relationships through the work of clergy like Frank Amery and Peter Barnett and our contact with the Caldmore churches and COMEX.

It was through this network that I was able to get names of contact people from each of the main faith communities in Walsall and be introduced to them. Wherever I have been involved in interfaith work, I have always built on the work of other people who have gained the trust of faith communities by helping them when they have encountered difficulties such as obtaining premises, planning permission, meeting their community needs. We set a date for a meeting in St Michael's church hall, Caldmore, which was considered 'safe territory' as the vicar, Revd Peter Barnett was trusted and respected by the faith communities and the church hall was regularly hired for social functions by Asian groups. Peter chaired that first meeting and later developments could not have happened without his groundwork and support and that of people like Revd Frank Amery.

We met one November evening in 1981, a little nervously, as we did not know who would turn up. We provided light refreshments at the beginning as people arrived, in order to give time to talk informally and relax a little. At this stage we were probably all a bit apprehensive, but we were greatly encouraged by a good turn out and the obvious interest from members of the Muslim, Sikh, Hindu and Christian communities.

I had sought the help of Ivy Gutteridge, secretary of the Wolverhampton Interfaith Group, and she had arranged to bring some Wolverhampton members to the Walsall meeting. There were Muslim, Sikh, Hindu and Black Pentecostal Christian representatives who spoke of their experience of the Wolverhampton Group. It was interesting that they all spoke of their early reservations about interfaith involvement, fearing a compromising of their beliefs. However, without exception, they spoke of how the encounter with people of other faith traditions strengthened their faith as they became more aware of what was important to them. They felt that they had become better Muslims, Sikhs, Hindus or Christians through the encounter with those of other faith traditions.

After hearing these experiences we asked the Walsall representatives if they thought a Walsall Interfaith Group was a good idea. There was an enthusiastic response and the Sikh representatives offered their premises for the first meeting.

We met at the local Sikh Gurdwara three weeks later on a very cold mid-December evening. Snow and ice made travelling treacherous. Vivien described it as 'the sort of night you wouldn't put a dog out', and we did not expect many people to come. To our surprise and delight nearly thirty people turned up, a good representation from the main faith communities in Walsall. The enthusiasm had not abated and it was further warmed by the generosity of Sikh hospitality.

We spent the evening being shown round the Gurdwara and enjoying tea and tasty snacks. Questions on Sikh practice were answered and we shared our ideas and hopes for the future. It was decided that we should meet monthly at one another's places of worship, taking it in turns to host the meeting. We would use the time to give each faith community an opportunity to explain something of its belief and practice. The meetings would focus on 'Who we are, what we do and why we do it'. The community offering the venue would be responsible for planning the programme and providing the speakers. We were not wanting academic lectures, rather an account of what it was like to be a Muslim, Sikh or Hindu in Walsall. We wanted to hear each other's stories. To stress the equality of all members in the group we agreed that the chairperson for each meeting should come from the community hosting the meeting. I volunteered to act as secretary to keep a record and send out notices of future meetings.

During the year of 1982 we met once a month except during August and we visited the main faith communities in Walsall which were Sikh, Muslim, Hindu and Christian. My work that year consisted of getting on my bike and making many visits to homes and places of worship to explore what was desirable and possible. I spent many hours at different services of worship, encountering much that was strange and often incomprehensible when the worship was in a language I did not understand.

My inability to understand intellectually allowed the more intuitive, feeling part of me to receive and explore the new experiences. I felt profoundly the atmosphere and spirit of worship, a sense of the reverence and devotion of the worshippers and their deep sense of community. I did experience a sense of confusion while being bombarded with so many new ideas and concepts and I was having to question many of my deeply-held assumptions. The security of my life in community, with the regular pattern of daily worship, prayer, silence and reflection, gave me a firm base from which to explore this new world. Wearing the habit of a religious sister meant that I was always dressed appropriately with a long enough skirt and my head covered with a veil. It was unmistakably clear who I was and what I stood for and I was received with the respect given to a dedicated person which was very humbling. One Muslim friend said to me when arranging a visit to a Mosque. 'You are all right because you are wearing the hijab!' My feelings in response to this remark were rather mixed but I made no comment.

I found that many communities were willing to host a meeting and that there would be a very good attendance from the host community, but people were far less willing to 'play away'. Long histories of conflict between some groups and continuing conflict in other places of the world made it difficult for some people to meet, although as the relationships of trust developed, we found it increasingly important to continue meeting while people in other parts of the world were at each other's throats.

The question of an appropriate venue was a difficult one. Should one choose a neutral venue? Does such a thing exist? On the whole we favoured visiting the different faith communities who were willing to host a meeting since that gave people a chance to experience the atmosphere and ethos of a faith community, and the people speaking felt more secure to share their experience on home ground. What was wanted was a real encounter between people of faith and the difficulties of language and custom were at least partly overcome by a glimpse of the spirit of a faith tradition.

I remember my first visit to a Hindu Temple. I entered the Temple aware of my prejudices and I felt in a very strange and almost alien atmosphere. I had been told that Hindus do not worship many gods and accepted that intellectually but I still felt enormous difficulty with the many statues. They 'felt' like idols to me and I was distinctly uncomfortable watching devotees bowing before them and offering gifts of flowers and fruit. Then my attention was caught by the sight of a woman approaching the lingam or phallus, a symbol of Shiva. Shiva is part of the divine triad who share the activities of Ishvara, the one supreme God who symbolizes Brahman, the Absolute. The power to create belongs to Brahma, preservation is the power of Vishnu and Shiva is the great destroyer. Although destroyer of life, Shiva is also the great recreator, in him is both ceaseless activity and eternal rest. He is often portrayed as king of the dancers, his dance speaking of the rhythm at the heart of all existence.

As I watched this woman approach the lingam with a milk bottle I caught a glimpse of the spirit of Hinduism. She poured

the milk over the lingam and I saw some one who was worshipping with her whole being. Her body and attitude was one
of total, selfless attention and I realized that I was on holy
ground. This experience challenged my prejudices and I began
to see what was going on around me in a new way. It was as if
scales had fallen from my eyes and I began to see something of
the beauty and wisdom of the faith traditions which I was
witnessing. I have to say here that to speak of Hinduism is also
inaccurate since that is a Western term imposed on a great
variety of Eastern traditions.

This experience is an example of how what we see is always
filtered through our previously received experience. When I
entered that Temple I was very limited in what I was able to
see since I was afraid of so much that was strange. I had not
experienced anything like it before and it was all very threatening until I saw something which resonated with my own experience. The sight of the woman totally absorbed in worship
touched something deep within me, I related to her desire
although she was using very strange symbols. My spirit reached
out to her spirit and we were drawn together in a basic human
desire to worship and communicate with the Divine. This
insight gave me some familiar ground on which to stand and I
was then able to see what was going on around me in a new
light.

At the end of the first year the Walsall Interfaith Group
consisted of a network of fifty to sixty people. The attendance
at the monthly meetings varied from fifteen to thirty people.
Some teachers and social workers were interested to receive
accounts of the meetings although they were not able to attend
meetings. The Interfaith Group became a resource for schools
and organizations when they needed a contact with a faith community over a particular issue or problem. The rapid growth of
this group was a reflection of the good community involvement
on the part of several churches and the longstanding tradition of
ecumenical co-operation. Most of the activity centred around
Caldmore since the Roman Catholic, Anglican, Methodist and
United Reformed churches in that area were used to working

together and the interfaith dimension was a natural development of their community involvement. The Interfaith Group flourished because of a core group of deeply committed people and my community allowed me to spend much of my time on this work.

The role of a secretary and convener of the meetings is crucial and it does take a lot of time to build up relationships. I received a useful tip from the secretary of the Wolverhampton Group. Ivy told me how, in their early days, members of the Wolverhampton Group delivered the minutes and notices of meetings by hand since the contacts between meetings were so crucial for the building up of relationships. I followed this model on many occasions which meant that I visited many homes and got to know the families. It took a lot of time since I was always offered refreshments but I learnt so much in the process. I still believe that it was some of the best-used time in my life.

There were language barriers and it was evident that the deep things of the heart and spirit did not easily translate into another language. Not only that, translation involves different world views and thought patterns and some concepts simply do not translate. Sometimes I was aware, when a misunderstanding arose, it was due to the same word being used in different ways. That is why it is so important to visit the places of worship and let people explain themselves on their home ground. I remember well a meeting when we had rather a dry academic lecture on Hinduism by someone who was rather sceptical. Towards the end of the meeting another Hindu, obviously frustrated, stood up and poured his heart out in his own language. His face shone and we felt the passion of conviction although most of us did not understand a single word. In spite of that we caught a glimpse of the spirit of his tradition.

When we met to assess our first year and plan for the future, we reflected on our growing understanding of our differences, our appreciation and respect for the distinctiveness of each faith tradition and awareness of how much we had in common. We were of one mind about the value of the venture and wanted to continue. We agreed to continue the pattern of our monthly meetings, taking it in turns to host the meeting and provide chairperson and speakers. I continued the secretarial support with help from a school secretary who typed the minutes and a Sikh friend who ran off copies on his duplicating machine. One day when I called on him to deliver the stencils he was obviously hard pressed. Heaving a big sigh he said, 'I am looking forward very much to the next life. This one is so full of trials.' 'Yes,' I said sympathetically. 'That will be the best interfaith group meeting of the lot!'

There was a moment's silence and we looked at each other in delight as we realized what I had said. I had spoken without thinking but it was from my heart and represented what I believed. Suddenly the whole concept of life beyond death became real and very attractive and I realized that the growing relationships of trust and friendship were indeed a foretaste of the Kingdom of God.

Later the typing was done by a Youth Employment scheme at Comex House and photocopying made the whole process much easier but there was something very special about those early days. They involved a great deal of pedal power and time but although the work took longer there were more everyday human contacts. By the end of that year my community had invested in a Honda 70 for my use. There was some opposition on my home ground to this move since it required some adaption to my habit to ensure safety. When I defended the change by saying I was getting exhausted by the mileage I was having to do on the bicycle, a friend said, 'Maureen, it is not going to reduce your workload. You will simply do more work if you can get around more quickly.' Words of truth!

It was thought helpful by some people, particularly the Christian clergy, to have a programme for the year so that they had good notice of meetings and could put them in their diaries. However, we were working in a great mixture of cultures and not every one kept a diary. I soon learnt the optimum time for sending out reminders of the meetings and who needed a phone call a couple of days before a meeting. It was not because they were not interested. They just operated on a different time schedule and this needed to be respected. There were plenty of tensions and frustrations in working in such a mix of cultures but the golden rule was – *do not be in a hurry*. This was a great challenge to someone who liked to get on with things and see results, but I soon learnt that relationships of trust cannot be manipulated or hurried. I valued and admired the time given to the exchange of courtesies before conducting business although I have often been slow to learn from the experience.

6

Growing Friendships

There was one person in particular who was to be the means of challenging my assumptions. Dilbagh Singh Mavi, a leading member of the Sikh community, became a very special friend. Dilbagh had been a local councillor for three years and was at that time chairman for the Commission for Racial Equality in the Midlands. Although leading a very active life he would meditate for a couple of hours when he came home each evening. When we first came to Walsall, advised by Revd Peter Barnett, vicar of St Michael's Church, Caldmore, we had sent a letter of introduction to key people in the Borough introducing ourselves and giving our daily timetable of prayer times. Dilbagh had responded with a warm welcome, particularly noting with delight our prayer times.

Dilbagh came to visit us in our council house. He arrived on the doorstep in his flowing white robes and blue turban and carefully removed his shoes as he crossed the threshold. We exchanged the traditional greeting with hands together and the little bow. We produced tea and biscuits and as we settled down I anticipated polite conversation. Dilbagh immediately started asking me about my prayer life. This I found more than a little daunting and I felt way out of my depth. Playing for time I pointed out that his tea was getting cold but he said, 'Never mind, I have come to talk about more important things.' I have never gone into such depths with anyone so quickly. Here was a man who sought God with a passionate love and devotion. Seeking God was the passion of his life and it showed not only in his demeanour but also in his lifestyle. He was a full-time teacher and a prominent leader in his community. He lived to serve.

As the conversation proceeded, I said, 'You are using the language of one of our great Christian mystics, St John of the Cross.' Dilbagh wanted to know more about St John's teaching than I was able to tell him. Later when visiting the convent in Essex I related this story to Sister Susanna, who although elderly and frail, took a great interest in what the younger sisters were doing. She was absolutely fascinated by my description of Dilbagh and offered me an abridged edition of St John's teaching to give to him. When I met him two or three weeks later he greeted me with a radiant smile. 'That book is a hundred per cent true, a hundred per cent true.' I was left feeling that he understood St John of the Cross far better than I did.

After our tea, we took Dilbagh upstairs to our chapel. Gill had made a beautiful altar frontal for the Easter season and 'Alleluya' was written across it. At once he said, 'That word. It is a wonderful word. Do you use it as a mantra? That is all you need. If you recite that word every day you will find God.' When he left a deep silence and peace remained in the house. We did our washing up very quietly. Gill eventually put our feelings into words. 'I feel that we have just had a visit from a very holy person.'

As our friendship developed so I came to have a deeper and deeper respect for this wonderful man. I would frequently visit his home and we shared the teachings of our respective scriptures. I gave him a Good News version of the New Testament and asked if there were any parts of the Guru Granth Sahib in English which I could borrow. I soon realized that I had made a major request. Sometime later when I visited he told me that he had a copy of the Holy Book for me to borrow and asked me where I would keep it. It should be kept in a place where there was no alcohol or meat. Having satisfied him that I would keep the book in chapel I was sent off to wash my hands before he put it into my hands to take home. It had been wrapped in a beautifully embroidered white cloth before being placed in a bag. I bore it home with great reverence.

This made a deep impression upon me and I observed the Sikh custom of taking off my shoes and washing my hands before I touched the Holy Book. I noticed how this affected my approach to reading those scriptures. The preparation by those physical acts helped to prepare my mind. I was aware of a greater openness and reverence for what I was reading.

My friendship with Dilbagh was one of the things which most influenced me while I was in Walsall. His face and his eyes held a special light which was difficult to describe. Both his demeanour and his actions spoke of a man who walked with God. I remember unwittingly putting the cat among the pigeons in a discussion group at a clergy conference. We had been asked to describe what we thought to be the marks of a spirit-filled person. As I struggled to put my thoughts into words a picture of Dilbagh's face came into my mind. 'The marks are openness, joy and peace and a sense of light – and I have seen it in a Sikh!' This produced heated argument as some thought I was being sentimental and unbiblical. I was rather bemused by the fallout but the wonder of my experience of that holy man could not be taken from me.

Shabbir Hussain was a member of the local mosque and very supportive of the Interfaith Group. I was always most welcome at his home and if he was not around I was entertained by his daughter who was in the sixth form of her local comprehensive school. From her I learned a great deal about the difficulties and tensions experienced by a Muslim young woman. When she first decided to wear the hijab or scarf at school it was a commitment of deep religious significance. Although she encountered ridicule and opposition she felt that as a devout Muslim woman that was how she wanted to express her obedience to Allah. She wore it with pride in her identity and faith tradition.

Her father obviously thought that I was a good role model for young people and asked me to meet the young Muslim women's group. Some were very shy and nervous of speaking with me but I did get an insight into their culture and way of life. These young girls were happy with their tradition and accepted as natural that their fathers would escort them to any events they attended. I later learnt, when sitting in on a workshop at a Muslim women's conference, that they distinguished between cultural and fundamentalist Muslims. They wanted to be known as fundamentalist Muslims as that meant adhering to the fundamentals of their faith. This alerted me to the care needed over use of words since the stereotype of a fundamentalist Muslim produced by the media is something quite different, about which my Muslim friends are equally unhappy.

I often met with Shabbir for a meal or a cup of tea and while sitting together in peaceful companionship he suddenly asked me, 'Sister, why do you not marry? You would have such devout children.' I was certainly taken aback by his words. It opened up the gulf of our different understanding. I tried to explain the meaning of my vow of celibacy, giving me greater freedom for God's work, but he obviously thought that the better way was to marry and have children. It reminded me of the moment when I told the student nurses in Zimbabwe why I was returning to England. When I told them that I was joining a religious order they gasped in horror. 'You can't do that. It says in the Bible be fruitful and multiply and you will be disobedient to God if you become a nun!'

For me friendship is one of God's greatest gifts. Having made the traditional vows of poverty, celibacy and obedience within a religious order, friendship, both within and outside my community, has been crucial in enabling me to grow and flourish as a human person. My time in Walsall was one in which, freed from the restrictions of institutional life, I was able to develop friendships with a very wide variety of people and for this reason the Walsall years were those of considerable spiritual and psychological growth.

Friendship is the very basis of our life as Christians. Jesus said, 'I do not call you servants any longer . . . but I have called you friends . . .' (John 15. 15). It is to this unbelievably daring relationship with God that we are invited. It is both an invitation and a challenge. 'This is my commandment, that you love one another as I have loved you' (John 15. 12), and lest we should try and spiritualize that command, Jesus gave us a concrete example as a preface to this teaching in John 13. 1–15. The story of Jesus washing the disciples' dusty, sweaty feet shows a spontaneous expression of human service and friendship which is in danger of being lost as we cast it into the stones of a Maundy Thursday liturgy. Instead of being a challenge to simple, earthy, natural service of each other's humanity it can become a pious and possibly manipulative ceremony of an 'in group'.

Friendship which is healthy is open and non-manipulative. It is a relationship enjoyed for its own sake. True friendship enlarges horizons and draws others into its orbit. In my community our rule warns us of the danger of exclusive relationships as they are destructive of community life. Exclusive relationships are also destructive of the people involved, since prejudices and blind spots tend to be reinforced. Groups which only allow in the like-minded and promote fellowship at the expense of healthy conflict can end up very stunted in their human development. I have a friend who very aptly calls them PLUDS. (People like us dear!)

My relationship with God grew and matured alongside my deepening relationships with friends from other faith traditions. The one nourished the other so that I have found it impossible to separate them. It was a real experience that we were bound up together and that we could not develop as mature humans apart from each other. It was very much the case of experiencing the 'Go-Between God', described by Bishop John V. Taylor in his book of that title, as the concrete foundation of our life together. I came to see that we were all on the same human journey and agreed on the basic requirements for that journey. Our friendship centred very much around hospitality; it was in our eating and talking together that we celebrated our joy and gratitude for life and creation and shared our concerns about all that marred these gifts of God.

Life is about relationships, the relationship with ourselves, each other, the environment and God, and it is the development and balance of all those relationships which makes for healthy human living. The Christian gospel is an invitation to fullness of life, therefore the nourishment of all those relationships must be the focus for Christian mission.

I discovered the energy that comes through celebration and how the encounters with friends of other faith traditions deepened my understanding of the richness within my own. We all have a tendency to be selective about the aspects of our faith tradition to which we give most attention, and one of the very challenging aspects of interfaith dialogue is that in listening to another person's story I am often confronted by an aspect of my own tradition which I have conveniently forgotten. This is why we need each other so much, to correct our distortions and bring a greater wholeness to our discipleship.

I was conscious of a very creative oscillation between my experience of other faith traditions and my experience as a Christian within my own faith community. It was brought home to me how much celebration is part of the Gospel stories and how many parties there are in them. Recently, sitting in church with my Jewish friend, Karen, the preacher remarked on how Jesus loved parties. 'Of course he did,' she whispered. 'He was a good Jew.'

The interfaith encounter would deepen and freshen my understanding of the Gospel stories and further pondering upon them in prayer would increase my openness to new insights in subsequent interfaith encounters. One great lesson I have received is about preparation for worship. Of course this is taught in the Christian tradition and one of the great pieces of wisdom in the teaching of Ignatius Loyola is that before prayer one stands a little way apart from one's prayer place and for a few moments thinks about what one is about to do and who one is coming to meet. Observing that practice has brought new life and depth to my prayer.

Muslims, Buddhists, Sikhs and Hindus all remove their shoes before entering the worship area. Sikhs will have a bath before coming to morning prayer and wash hands after removing shoes before entering the prayer hall. Muslims perform 'Wudu' or ablutions before each prayer time. The preparation of the body profoundly affects our attitude of mind as I discovered when observing Sikh practice before reading the Guru Granth Sahib. Moses' experience before the burning bush expresses a basic human response to the sense of the holy. 'Remove the sandals from your feet, for the place on which you are standing is holy ground' (Ex. 3 .5).

As I entered a place of worship in another tradition, the act of removing my shoes impinged upon my mind. I was approaching holy ground, the experience of the Divine for my Sikh, Muslim or Hindu friends. I came with reverence as I approached what is holy and precious to them and my openness to them and my openness to God were one movement. I have found that the most creative visits have been when I have been able to suspend my intellectual questionings and just receive the experience without value judgments, comparisons or theological questionings. These are best left until after the visit for prayerful reflection, alone or with others. By this I am not compromising my own beliefs, I am firmly rooted in my own tradition but temporarily I suspend judgment and receive. It is a deeply contemplative attitude and is nourished by faithfulness to the discipline of my own religious tradition.

I have found that the daily discipline of my prayer time with the stillness and openness to God which I endeavour to nourish and my openness and reverence for the experience of my Muslim and Sikh friends are inextricably linked. One feeds the other and through this I am nourished and opened up to the incredibly wonderful diversity of life and human experience which I believe to be a reflection of our Christian understanding of God as Trinity. At this time in Walsall new horizons were appearing and my journey through life was being greatly enriched by the companionship of my friends of other faith traditions.

7

How Much Can We Do Together?

It is written into the rule of my community that a sister be prepared to travel, at the shortest notice, to any place. This was particularly applicable when we worked in Tanzania and had many small mission houses to staff. In the event of emergencies and sickness a sister could be asked to pack her few belongings into one suitcase and go to help out at very short notice. At the end of July 1982 Gill was asked by the Reverend Mother to return to the convent in Essex in order to work in the Hospital and Homes of Saint Giles, and Gloria came to take Gill's place.

There was considerable concern at the convent about what the Walsall sisters were doing, going into temples and mosques. I later learnt that as Gloria prepared for the move she said, 'I'm not going into any temple or mosque and taking my shoes off!'

I knew nothing about this and the day after Gloria arrived I announced that on the coming Saturday I was invited by Mr Toor, president of the Pleck Sikh Temple, to the wedding of his niece. The invitation included Gloria as I had told Mr Toor that she was coming to Talke Road. I thought Gloria looked a bit perplexed, although she said nothing. I told her that she was very welcome but if she did not want to come she would be at home all day on her own.

Gloria decided to come with me and we walked to the Gurdwara in the Pleck, Walsall. I said little to her except to explain the basic rules of etiquette. For Gloria it was all rather overwhelming as it was only her third day in Walsall and she had not met many people. It was a case of being thrown in at the deep end. Her first impression was of the friendliness of everyone. We received a wonderful welcome and were offered refreshments when we arrived and a Sikh woman from Kent came and sat next to Gloria and looked after her for the rest of the proceedings.

We were present to witness the Betrothal Ceremony or exchange of gifts between the families before the wedding ceremony. This can happen at the homes of the bridegroom and bride some time before the wedding and is a solemn binding engagement between the couple. After tea the bride and bridegroom, along with their relatives and friends, entered the prayer hall. Both parties sat together and listened to Keertan, the singing of sacred hymns. The groom took his seat facing the Guru Granth Sahib, then the bride came, led by her brother and friends and took her place by the groom on the left side.

There were prayers and a reading from the Holy Book followed a sermon from the person officiating. The girl's father placed one end of the bridegroom's long scarf into the hand of his daughter, thus giving her away. Then during the singing of the marriage hymns from the Guru Granth Sahib, the bridegroom led the bride round the Holy Book seven times, the bride holding on to the end of his scarf. The four verses of the Laavan or marriage hymns describe the development and consolidation of marital love and at the same time, the love and longing of the human soul for God.

The culmination of the ceremony was the opening of the Holy Book and the reading of a verse at random, after which Kraah Prashaad was distributed to all present. (This is customary at the end of most religious ceremonies and is described in chapter 3.) After the religious ceremony we went downstairs for Langar, the shared meal, which was particularly delicious on this special occasion. Here Gloria discovered for herself the wonderful generosity of Sikh hospitality.

It was late afternoon when we got home. It had been a powerful experience and a long day and we were both tired. Impressions were left to simmer. I did notice that from that day there was no problem about Gloria joining in with the activities of the Interfaith Group. Later, she told me that it seemed quite natural to take one's shoes off when going into the Gurdwara.

Dilbagh Mavi had not been able to attend the wedding and it was several weeks before Gloria met him in the Sikh Temple. He delighted in Gloria's name. He always pronounced it with a particular intonation which made it sound a word of praise. Gloria took Gill's place as an assistant hospital chaplain at the Manor Hospital and often met Dilbagh in the course of her travelling or in the hospital itself. It was always a lift to her day when she met him. She says that she not only found him very friendly but there was also something very special about him. He had a quiet, spiritual dignity and there was something distinctive about his eyes: something which could not be put into words and it was there whatever he was talking about, be it the weather or his work at school. Gloria thought it was a mark of holiness.

As the Walsall Interfaith Group developed, we discovered how much we could do together without compromising our respective beliefs. Deep friendships were developing, based on mutual trust and respect. Most of the activity centred around the districts of Caldmore and Palfrey and built upon the community involvement of the churches.

Walsall consists of many villages which have merged into each other as they have grown. However, each district has still kept its own sense of identity and it is even possible to recognize a difference in accent in the speech of people from north and south Walsall. The population of Caldmore is very mixed with a large Afro-Caribbean community and Palfrey next door had a very large Asian community. A local housing association has done a very great deal to provide good housing and so at that time there was a strong sense of belonging and feeling relatively good about the local area. A walk down the main street of Palfrey would reveal a variety of shops owned by Asian families with the tantalizing smell of aromatic spices in the air. Indeed, one of the first things I did when coming into the area was to call into one of the shops to have a lesson on curry making and how to use the various spices.

Under the leadership of an energetic headmistress, Palfrey Junior School was very involved in the local community and later it became what was known as a Community School. Local groups were able to apply for membership and use the facilities for evening and weekend events. The Walsall Interfaith Group became a member, as the school provided a very good venue for the social events of the group. St Michael's church hall in Caldmore was another venue which was widely used by local groups and therefore provided another good place for meetings. We found it best to hold our regular meetings in each other's places of worship and use Palfrey School or St Michael's church hall for the social events.

The meetings were as informal as possible. We avoided platforms and rows of seats and preferred to sit round in a circle to emphasize the equality of all participating. The light refreshments and informal conversation before the meetings were as important as the main meeting and also ensured that we had a good number when the main event of the evening began. Meeting in this way we discovered that, although we came from different cultures, histories and world views, we had the same basic human aspirations and concerns. We shared our concern about quality of life for ourselves and our families and children, about education and employment, security and the way society was developing. We were concerned about health and happiness and the search for meaning in life. It was this common human quest that united us beyond our different religious traditions. Indeed the purpose of a religious tradition was seen to be that of enabling us to be human.

Religious Education in schools was a key issue so we arranged a Day Conference one Saturday in January 1983 when representatives of the faith traditions in Walsall met together with several local teachers, tutors and students from the West Midlands College of Higher Education and the Schools Officer from the (Anglican) Lichfield diocese. The relevance of this issue was clearly shown by the attendance. We had nearly fifty people attending, with a large number coming from the Muslim, Sikh and Hindu communities. The Revd Michael Metcalf, who played a very important role in the development of the Interfaith Group, was chairman and introduced the morning session,

'What do we want in Religious Education?' He reminded us that the central purpose of the day was to enable us to listen to one another and seek to understand one another's point of view. There was a really good sharing of views, highlighting the concern that children be grounded in the faith tradition of their parents and that teachers in training be adequately prepared to teach in a multifaith setting. The age at which a child is taught about other faith traditions produced some conflict and some did not want it to happen until secondary school or even sixth form. Others thought that was quite unrealistic since children from the different faith traditions were together from the beginning of their school days. Learning about the main festivals could start at a very early age, with the more theological questions being left until much later. The importance of school visits to different places of worship was discussed and here useful contacts were made for the future arrangement of such visits.

In the afternoon, the General Inspector for Schools in Birmingham with special responsibility for RE shared some very helpful examples of what can be done using artefacts from the different faith traditions. He spoke on his experience of the new Agreed Syllabus in Birmingham and encouraged us in Walsall to work out what we wanted in RE. This was an important day and work on Religious Education in schools continued over the ensuing months and years, building on the foundation of the contacts made and understanding gained.

One World Week gave a good opportunity to organize events to celebrate the richness and diversity of our multifaith world. At this time in the 1980s One World Week and the Week of Prayer for World Peace occurred in the same week, the last full week in October, which included United Nation's Day, 24 October. In 1983 United Nations Day fell on a Sunday and we celebrated it by organizing a Faith Tour.

After morning service at St Michael's Church, Caldmore, a small group of Christians from the local churches, Anglican, Methodist, Roman Catholic and United Reformed met in the church hall for a shared picnic lunch. We then walked about a quarter of a mile to the Guru Nanak Sikh Temple where we were welcomed by the president and members of the Sikh community. We all covered our heads, removed our shoes and washed our hands. We were then escorted upstairs to the prayer hall where we had a short talk on Sikhism and prayers for peace were said by the priest. For most of the Christians present this was their first visit to the Gurdwara and the time was all too short to take in the richness of the experience. After prayers we went downstairs to be given refreshments and there was time for a few questions but we were not able to stay as long as we would have liked since we were visiting four places of worship that afternoon. This first glimpse of the richness of Sikh worship and the generosity and graciousness of their welcome encouraged some of the Christians to visit again.

Members of the Sikh community joined us as we walked through Caldmore to the mosque about half a mile away. The austerity of that building contrasted with the Gurdwara but again we found a very deep atmosphere of prayer. We again removed our shoes and the women in the group covered their heads as we entered the mosque. We received a very warm welcome from the Imam and members of the Muslim community. One member gave a short talk on Islam and another recited a few verses from the Qur'an. We heard about the five pillars of Islam. The first is the 'shahada' or witness, 'I bear witness that there is no god but Allah; I bear witness that Muhammad is his prophet.'

Islam means 'submission to God' and all one has to do to become a Muslim is to recite the 'shahada' in public. These are the first words breathed into a child's ear at birth and the last a Muslim will utter with his dying breath. The other pillars are the 'salat' or prayers five times daily; fasting during the month of Ramadan; Zakat, a compulsory tax on wealth; and the Hajj or pilgrimage to Mecca once in a life time for those with the health and financial resources to perform it.

There was time for a few questions and we were able to take note of the clocks on the wall indicating the current times for the five daily prayer times.

Fajr   dawn prayer
Zuhr   after mid-day prayer
Asr   late afternoon prayer
Maghrib   after sunset prayer
Isha   night prayer

We also saw a list of the prophets which included many figures familiar to Christians such as Ibrahim (Abraham), Isma'il (Ishmael), Ishaq (Isaac), Yaqoob (Jacob), Yusuf (Joseph), Musa (Moses), Daood (David), Sulayman (Solomon), Yahya (John the Baptist) and 'Isa (Jesus). Mohammed came at the end of the list as the final and greatest prophet. The line of prophets and the place of Jesus in that line raised sharp questions for Christians but we could do no more than take note at this point with the promise of more discussion in the future. Here we were confronted by a sharp conflict in belief. At this point we did not deny it, neither did we attempt to argue our different positions. We were content to acknowledge our differences and pay attention to that which we had in common, our desire to obey God and our search for true peace and better understanding between the faith traditions. Our pilgrimage that afternoon was a concrete expression of a commitment to further dialogue. Some of the members of the mosque continued with us as we then went to the Roman Catholic church nearby.

Here with the cold, stone floors we kept our shoes firmly on. Some Christians prepared themselves as they entered the church by dipping their finger in the holy water stoup and making a sign of the cross. This was a reminder of baptism and a very good way to prepare for prayer if Protestant sensibilities did not get in the way. We were welcomed by the parish priest who gave us a short history of the church and assured us of his support and encouragement for our venture. To show that this support was given by the whole of the Roman Catholic Church he read a short extract from a Papal Encyclical to that effect. Our Sikh and Muslim friends were fascinated by the splendour of the building, although the statues and figures in the stained glass windows presented a difficulty for the Muslims. Islam does not permit the representation of any living creature and the only decoration in mosques is Arabic script, which in large mosques is of quite stunning beauty. After prayers for peace we continued on our way.

By this time we numbered about forty people and we then walked a mile to St Matthew's Church at the top of the hill overlooking Walsall. We were welcomed by the vicar, Revd Roger Sainsbury (now Bishop of Barking) and again prayers for peace were said. Then we were invited into the vestry for what was the highlight of the afternoon for our Sikh and Muslim friends. We were given a short account of the history of the church and shown some very ancient baptism registers and a seventeenth-century chalice and paten. I well remember the shining eyes of one of my Sikh friends as we gazed at the ancient books. It gave me a new appreciation of the tradition to which I belong and the strength that lies within it. Seeing the response of my Sikh friend opened my eyes to the strength and value of belonging to a tradition with years of history. A sense of rootedness gave me a deeper sense of stability and I was encouraged by the thought of countless, ordinary Christians down the centuries struggling to be faithful in the face of their particular struggles and temptations.

At the end of the afternoon we had a cup of tea in the church hall with a time for questions and discussion. We had all been enriched by the afternoon. We had visited four places of worship and seen something of the richness of our respective traditions. This was a very modest venture early in the development of the Walsall Interfaith Group, but it was an important and formative event. It was local and involved local people who wanted to get to know their neighbours of faith. Representatives of the local places of worship were able to do something together and it strengthened our on-going relationships. We had seen more clearly some of our differences and were beginning to learn to live with them. I had experienced what many people do in interfaith encounters, a new appreciation for the richness of my own tradition.

We had walked together and prayed together. The conversations while walking from one place to another had developed and deepened friendships. Learning to walk together for a few hours can help us to walk together in our wider life experience. Having a common purpose strengthens our ability to walk together, to accept and respect our differences and feel more deeply the things we have in common.

8

Sharing Our Riches

Over the past two or three years we had shared hospitality, explained something of our beliefs and practices; we had walked and talked together and we had prayed. During the Faith Tour a member from each place of worship we visited prayed in his/her own way and the rest of us received the contribution in silence. In that silence we had stood together before the one God and prayed in our own way. We were united in seeking God and his purpose of peace. We were able to pray together. Our experience was that there are no barriers to faith.

Faith is not primarily about belief systems, it is about openness to God, about openness to life and each other. It is about a readiness to be changed by that experience, a willingness to live with the questions raised. Faith is something which unites us and is not the same thing as a belief system. I have an uncomfortable feeling that a belief system can actually be an obstacle to faith. That is why I want to refer to a religion as a faith tradition rather than a faith. The purpose of a faith tradition is to sow the seeds of faith and provide the fertile soil for their germination and nurture. That nurture is like a gestation period preparing for a mature faith to be born into a wider world, in order to grow to a deeper maturity alongside diverse life experiences and challenges. All too often a religious tradition, for a variety of reasons, can hold its adherents in immaturity and dependency so that faith never reaches maturity. It can then be used to reinforce and sanctify human prejudices and confirm racist and sectarian barriers. Faith can die stillborn if it does not mature alongside life experience and may often be jettisoned as unwanted baggage on life's journey.

During the Week of Prayer for World Peace, a vigil for Peace and Racial Justice was kept at St Michael's Church, Caldmore. This was an ecumenical Christian event and when we started the Interfaith Group we incorporated this vigil into our programme and extended an invitation to members of the other faith traditions in Walsall. We did not get a great response, understandably, since it was held in a Christian church, but the fact that it happened and that there was an open invitation was appreciated. A few members from the Sikh and Muslim communities came along late in the evening to see what was happening.

We continued to hold this vigil each year as part of the interfaith programme in One World Week and also arranged an event of a more social nature during that week. One year we chose for discussion the subject, 'The Contribution of Faith Communities to World Development and World Peace'. I looked forward to an enlightening evening which I duly got in a very succinct statement from our Hindu speaker. 'The world religions have contributed more to world war than world peace.' A sobering statement which left us all humbled and open to sharing ways of redressing that record.

As a result of this, in the following year (1985) we held a 'Peace Hour' in St Michael's church hall. Each faith tradition was asked to contribute a hymn, reading or prayer on the theme of peace. About forty of us sat round in a circle and the Sikhs set the tone by requesting that there be no applause after their singing since it was an act of worship not a performance. We therefore observed a time of silence after each contribution. The choir from the New Testament Church of God sang gospel songs, a group of Sikhs sang hymns from the Guru Granth Sahib accompanied by harmonium and drums, we had readings from the different scriptures and prayers for peace.

One very moving moment came when the Sikhs present all stood up and recited one of their chief prayers together. We were then given the following translation but the solemnity of the moment was in allowing the Punjabi words to float over us and feel the importance of that united prayer for them. It is a

prayer every Sikh child learns and is said at every service of
worship. It could be said to take the comparable place in Sikh
worship of the Lord's Prayer for Christians.

There is One God.
He is the supreme truth.
He, The Creator,
Is without fear and without hate.
He, the Omnipresent,
Pervades the universe.
He is not born
Nor does He die to be born again.
By His grace shalt thou worship Him.
Before time itself
There was truth.
When time began to run its course
He was the truth
And
Evermore shall truth prevail.

As the hour progressed so the atmosphere of reverence and
prayer deepened. We had not in any way ignored our differences or compromised our respective beliefs and practices, yet
we discovered a deep unity of spirit and ability to worship and
pray together. We had not set out to organize a joint service of
worship. We had come together with a common desire for peace
and this was the natural outcome of our growing friendship. We
were sensitively exploring together the way forward and in this
shared experience we found that we could pray together in a
way that preserved the integrity of all our faith traditions. Our
one sorrow was that our Muslim friends did not join us. They
have difficulty over the use of musical instruments and could
not recite the Qur'an in such circumstances. We could only
respect their views and keep in dialogue.

I have great difficulty with the attitude that we can do everything together except pray. As people of faith, to attempt to
sideline prayer is totally unrealistic. However there are import-

ant guidelines to observe. Any prayer together should not be
forced as if we just think that it is a good thing to do. It can
only happen with authenticity when it is a natural outcome for
people who have been working together. Then it is an appropriate expression of what has probably been going on silently
for some time. Each contribution from a faith tradition should
have space for silence around it to preserve the distinctiveness
and integrity of each tradition. We need to be clear as to what
we are doing. We are not 'all the same really'. That is to do a
grave injustice to the richness, value and beauty of every tradition. We need to come in a spirit of humility before God and
each other, open to the Holy Spirit and each other, confident
that in this spirit we will not go far astray.

An event which really brought the Interfaith Group to life
and involved many more people was an event in the 1988 One
World Week. We held a Festival of Talents, calling it 'Sharing
our Riches'. We asked people to bring along art and craft work
for sale or exhibition, food to sell or for the bring and share
supper and items for entertainment. It was an event which
produced interest from very many people. Members of the
group made offers of help or suggested friends who would be
interested. I visited many homes for the first time and Asian
women, unable to come to evening meetings because of small
children, made generous offers of food.

As always, on the night one never quite knew what or who
was going to turn up. There was hectic activity before the
meeting collecting promised items, and I turned up at the church
hall rather breathless to be confronted by a crowd of people
putting up pictures, displaying needlework, knitwear, painting
and carpentry. The colour, variety and beauty of work from the
different cultures was breathtaking. There were tapestries, saris,
embroidered table cloths, children's clothes. It really did express
the wonderful diversity of giftedness amongst the people of
Walsall. There was such a wonderful atmosphere. People were
proud of their contributions and excited by seeing them displayed. Conversation really flowed as they admired each other's
contributions and exclaimed over the expert needlework.

Church members were amazed at what others in their con-
gregations had done. They had not known that such talent
existed, so much had been hidden under the proverbial bushel.

This event crossed barriers in a way our more intellectual discussions could not. There was so much colour in the room as
there were many more women than usual, who were delighted
to bring along their produce. There was a happy sharing of
ideas and expertise and exchange of cooking recipes over the
shared vegetarian supper.

After supper there was a short time for entertainment when a
gospel choir sang and a Sikh woman sang hymns from the Guru
Granth Sahib. The exuberance of the gospel choir contrasted
well with the serene, quiet dignity of the Sikh hymns and again
it helped us to appreciate the rich diversity in our traditions.

The evening finished with the Story of the Rainbow, an
Indian Legend, which I read from the September 1986 copy of
Encounter produced by the Birmingham Multi-Faith Resource
Centre. Ancient people recognized the rainbow as a symbol of
peace and harmony. Ancient Hebrews recognized it as a special
sign given by God that God wants all living things to live and
flourish in peace and harmony. 'When the bow is in the clouds,
I will see it and remember the everlasting covenant between God
and every living creature of all flesh that is on the earth' (Gen.
9. 16).

Once upon a time, all the colours in the world started to
quarrel; each claiming she was the best, the most important,
the most useful, the favourite:

GREEN said: 'Clearly I am the most important. I am the
sign of life and of hope. I was chosen for the grass, trees,
leaves – without me all the animals would die. Look out over
the countryside and you will see that I am in the majority.'

BLUE interrupted: 'You only think about the earth, but
consider the sky and the sea. It is water that is the basis of life
and this is drawn up by the clouds from the blue sea. The sky
gives space and peace and serenity. Without my peace you
would all be nothing but busybodies.'

YELLOW chuckled: 'You are all so serious. I bring laughter, gaiety and warmth into the world. The sun is yellow, the moon is yellow, the stars are yellow. Every time you look at a sunflower, the whole world starts to smile. Without me there would be no fun.'

ORANGE started next to blow his own trumpet: 'I am the colour of health and strength. I may be scarce but I am precious for I serve the inner needs of human life. I carry all the most important vitamins. Think of carrots and pumpkins, oranges, mangoes and pawpaws. I don't hang around all the time but when I fill the sky at sunrise or sunset, my beauty is so striking that no one gives another thought to any of you.'

RED could stand it no longer. He shouted out: 'I'm the ruler of you all, blood, life's blood. I am the colour of danger and bravery. I am willing to fight for a cause. I bring fire in the blood. Without me the earth would be as empty as the moon. I am the colour of passion and love; the red rose, poinsettia and poppy.'

PURPLE rose up to his full height. He was very tall and he spoke with great pomp. 'I am the colour of royalty and power. Kings, chiefs, and bishops have always chosen me for I am a sign of authority and wisdom. People do not question me; they listen and obey.'

INDIGO spoke more quietly than all the others, but just as determinedly: 'Think of me. I am the colour of silence. You hardly notice me, but without me, you would all become superficial. I represent thought and reflection, twilight and deep waters. You need me for balance and contrast, for prayer and for inner peace.'

And so all the colours went on boasting, each convinced that they were the best. Their quarrelling became louder and louder. Suddenly, there was a startling flash of brilliant white lightning; thunder rolled and boomed. Rain started to pour down relentlessly. The colours all crouched down in fear, drawing close to one another for comfort.

Then RAIN spoke: 'You foolish colours, fighting among yourselves, each trying to dominate the rest. Do you not

know that God made you all each for a special purpose,
unique and different. He loves you all, he wants you all. Join
hands with one another and come with me. We will stretch
you across the sky in a great bow of colour, as a reminder
that he loves you all, that you can live together in peace; a
promise that he is with you – a sign of hope for tomorrow.'

The reading of this story was an appropriate way to end the
evening. It summed up our experience of that evening and the
preceding years. The variety of our histories, customs, symbols,
rituals and talents was like a glorious rainbow; and like the
rainbow, we need the experience of each other to show up the
beauty and richness of our own.

By this time the Walsall Interfaith Group had been meeting
for nearly seven years. Judging from my own experience I would
say that we had all grown both personally and as a group. The
interfaith experience was something that was enriching us on
many levels.

I had been both challenged and inspired by the devotion and
faithfulness of my Sikh, Muslim and Hindu friends. There was
an atmosphere of deep respect and questions were asked so
courteously. We had been meeting for about five years before
we had any sharp exchange of opinions. We felt that was a sign
of growing closer together. It was becoming safe to disagree.

My friends' reverence in approaching holy things and the
atmosphere of temple and mosque did make me want to take off
my shoes, as I knew myself to be on holy ground. The required
courtesies before starting any activity did bring home to me
the divine presence in other people and I was learning to enjoy
people for their own sake. The differences became characteris-
tics of people I had come to love and I did not want to change
them. I found myself to be delighted, challenged, inspired,
energized; given a wider vision and a deeper hope in the loving
purpose of God.

9

Final Days in Walsall

While I was involved in all this interfaith work the building of the sheltered accommodation and day centre for the elderly and disabled with the convent for the sisters had been progressing slowly, with many delays. In June 1984 the Bishop of London, Dr Graham Leonard, came to open and bless the new building. There had been a frantic scramble to be ready for that day and the sisters were still not able to move in to their convent next door to St Gabriel's Church, Fullbrook. Eventually, about two months later, we were able to move from Talke Road into our convent above the Day Centre. It was a very compact building in pleasant surroundings and very much quieter than Talke Road. When the winter came we were to discover its further advantages, snug in our draught free, centrally-heated home. But we had lost our close neighbours and with the inevitable intercom system at the entrance, people did not find us as accessible. The children we knew visited once out of curiosity but did not come again. They were growing up anyway and had other interests. I probably found it hardest to adjust and always remember Talke Road with great affection. It was very strange to go back as a visitor and eventually visit the people who moved into our former home.

We were now responsible as the wardens of the flats at nights, weekends and public holidays. This was a tie but there were now five sisters in the convent and four of us could share those duties. So we were still able to continue our wider involvements. Gill returned to take up hospital chaplaincy again and Gloria started a club for the disabled. Vivien was now at our convent at Effingham in Surrey and Barbara Mary joined us and visited people in the local parish. Sister Grace Mary was rather disabled with arthritis but her prayerful presence and interest in each one of us when we came home was a wonderfully stabilizing influence. She also visited in the flats and the residents valued her gentle presence and friendship enormously.

The garden shed was moved from Talke Road and provided shelter for my Honda 70 and I was once again mobile and continued the interfaith work. The effect of the Walsall Interfaith Group extended far beyond the organized meetings. There were many chance meetings in the streets or shops, on the bus or train. The sharing of news of our families, the sharing of anniversaries and festivals all deepened our friendship. I remember Dilbagh Mavi's interest when my mother came to visit for a few days. He came to see her and put himself at her service to drive her to any place she wanted to visit. He took her to Birmingham coach station at the end of her visit and drove us the long way through the Sandwell Valley so that she could appreciate the view. When we arrived at the coach station he insisted that I stayed with her until the coach left and as there was some delay, he had to drive around the block many times. I was most embarrassed by the delay but he was totally unruffled.

At the time of the storming of the Golden Temple at Amritsar there was considerable tension between Hindus and Sikhs. On the Friday evening a petrol bomb was thrown at the Hindu Temple in Caldmore and, although it was reported that white youths were seen running away, tension between the Sikh and Hindu communities was escalating and the atmosphere was electric. It was feared that it would not take much to ignite a serious incident.

Clergy from the Anglican and Methodist churches in Caldmore, Mike Sears, Francis Palmer and Frank Amery, arranged a visit both to the Sikh Gurdwara and the Hindu Temple on the Sunday morning, which happened to be Pentecost. They arrived at the Gurdwara during morning prayers and sat with the Sikh community for a while, praying in silence. After a while one of the members approached them, saying that there would be a gap in the service shortly and they would like one of the clergy to say a few words. It was decided that Francis would stay behind to speak while Mike and Frank went on to the Hindu Temple.

Francis spoke briefly to over two hundred Sikhs, explaining why the clergy had come to visit and pray and the other two had left to go on to the Hindu Temple. That talk on reconciliation, translated into Punjabi, was the only sermon that Francis gave that Pentecost Sunday. There was a distinct air of Pentecost about that incident, of different cultures and languages brought together by a common concern for truth, peace and justice under the One God.

One evening Dilbagh Mavi, accompanied by three other members of the local Sikh community, arrived on Francis Palmer's doorstep in great distress. A faithful Sikh had just been convicted of conspiracy to murder. While he had been on remand, food, prepared by members of his community, had been brought into him. However, now that he was convicted, this was no longer permitted and he was going to have to eat the food put before him. This he was refusing to do. 'It has been prepared by people who smoke and drink,' he said, 'and I will not touch it.' So he was in effect on hunger strike and his family were extremely worried.

Francis, on hearing the story, made two phone calls in the presence of these Sikh friends so that they could hear all that was being said. The first call was to the bishop responsible for prisons, Bishop Hardy, and the other call was to London. Having alerted the authorities to what was happening, Francis said, 'There is no more I can do. All we can do now is pray,' and the Christian and four Sikhs stood and prayed together in silence.

A week later, Dilbagh rang Francis to say, 'It is all right now. Your prayers have been answered.' '*Our* prayers,' replied Francis.

Ethel Hinton, a Steward at Caldmore Methodist Church, had been brought up in Corporation Street near to the Methodist Church and her parents made a habit of looking after elderly people in the street. Ethel and her brother, Stan, continued this care after the death of their parents. However, Ethel often wondered who would look after them when they became old.

Ethel tells of the good relationships and real community spirit present in Caldmore. Good relationships between Christians and members of the local mosque were started by the Revd Frank Amery during his time as minister at Caldmore Methodist Church and built on by the Walsall Interfaith Group. Before the building of the mosque the Muslims only had a small building and so hired the Methodist church hall for festivals such as Eid. Now that they have a purpose built mosque the Muslims do not need to use the hall and they offer the use of the mosque car park to the Methodists as their car park is very small. 'Don't ask, Ethel,' says the Imam. 'Just use it. It is yours.'

Ethel speaks most warmly about her Muslim neighbours. 'They are really wonderful. Last year my brother and I had a very rough year. I contracted shingles and then three weeks later my brother had a stroke. That Sunday evening my Muslim neighbour, Sargid, went with us in the ambulance to the hospital and stayed with me until 3.30 am and then brought me home. My Muslim neighbours were absolutely wonderful to me during that difficult time. I thank God for my Muslim friends, they are so kind and helpful.'

There is a very closely-knit local community in that area of Caldmore, friendly and considerate in so many ways. Ethel was carrying a large bucket of flowers from her house to the church and a Muslim friend rushed out of his shop to carry them for her. Anything she carries which looks the least bit heavy elicits this response. She is sometimes invited to special events at the mosque and is now in the process of arranging a meeting with members of the mosque for some church members who are wanting to know more about Islam and develop a better understanding. There are countless stories of friendship and neighbourliness happening very quietly as part of normal life in such areas as Caldmore.

The Walsall years were for me very rich years and I was wonderfully supported in my explorations by my sisters and many of my Christian friends. However, I have to say that not all my experience in relating to people in the churches has been happy. I felt myself very marginalized at times.

'How is your social work?' asked one priest, and I couldn't help feeling that I was somehow a second-class sister, since in his eyes I was not doing spiritual work and preaching the gospel.

Syncretism was another word thrown at me. This is a term referring to the merging of different schools of thought and beliefs, and is a fear which makes some Christians hesitant of getting involved in interfaith dialogue. I have never advocated syncretism since I value and delight in the distinctiveness of each faith tradition, although I do acknowledge that all religious traditions are influenced in their development by the thought patterns and practices which surround them.

'I don't believe in giving them an inch,' said one angry priest when I tried to explain myself. I was left feeling so sad at an insecurity which could only see one's identity over against those who are different, as if there was only so much space for us all and our differences meant that there was a shortage of space. What sort of God created a world like that? Not the God I was discovering and coming to love passionately. The God who is utterly beyond human understanding, whose purpose of love is beyond our wildest dreams; the God who is creating an expanding universe, the myriads of stars and galaxies, the great mountains I saw in Africa, the mighty Victoria Falls, vast deserts and the bush veldt in which I loved to walk. The God who upholds the life of the tiniest insect and the beautiful flower, the God who not so much paints the flowers of the poets but one who 'lets be' and so releases the fascinating and terrible process of evolution. This is a God who is vulnerable because so much power is given into human hands and we have such a capacity to spoil and destroy this wonderful creation.

As a Christian I believe that this vulnerability of God was particularly shown in the person of Jesus Christ who demonstrated God's risk in sharing with us God's work of creation and redemption. In the Gospel stories we see Jesus intimately in touch with creation and human processes, who must have had a winning personality in order to attract such a variety of people to associate with him.

The accusation, 'Look, a glutton and a drunkard, a friend of tax collectors and sinners' (Luke 7.34) tells us so much about the character of Jesus. He was such good company and able to be at home with all sorts of people. He scandalized the religious people of his day by the people with whom he kept company. I get a picture of parties with plenty of loud laughter of which religious people definitely did not approve.

Jesus showed the hospitality of God, the God who welcomes and invites, who offers unbelievable gifts and the total freedom to refuse. Jesus was continually crossing boundaries, the boundary between the respectable rabbi and the marginalized in society, the unattached man and unrelated women, the Jew and the Gentile, the colonized Jew and the Roman colonizer. His intimate relationship with the Father showed him that there were no barriers to God's love and the welcome and purpose of God was for all. 'Welcome one another, therefore, just as Christ has welcomed you, for the glory of God' (Rom. 15.7).

It is this welcome we are to offer if we can make any claim to follow Christ. It is a welcome without conditions, a welcome that delights in the 'otherness' of the other, a welcome that invites all to participate in the human journey and supports the most faltering steps in that quest. A welcome which does not insist on a system of belief but does demand a faith that will be open to risk and surprise. As Bishop John V. Taylor once so wonderfully put it in a lecture at St Giles, London, 'Being able to stay with six fathoms of uncertainty beneath you.'

I have come to see that the gospel is about invitation, an invitation to a whole new way of living which is only possible through a new way of seeing. This new way of seeing, the seeing of ourselves, others, the world and God, is the gift that Jesus offers and it is both gift and demand. It will surpass our wildest hopes and dreams and demand everything we have got, taking us both into the most terrifying vulnerability and fulfilling our deepest desires. It is this vulnerability and fullness of human living that I believe God is calling us to as we approach the millennium.

In every generation this call of God is firmly rooted in material, social and political existence. At this moment in human history the presence of the great world faith traditions side by side is a challenge to them all. In a world of increasing mobility and speed of communication we can no longer ignore the presence of those who live by very different belief systems.

One world, many faiths? How are we going to live together in a way which will enhance our quality of life? Are we, like the colours in the legend of the rainbow, going to continue to argue as to who is the truest, the greatest, the best? Can we rather put our energies into learning to appreciate each other and support each other to be more faithful to the essence of our particular faith traditions? The experience of the Walsall Interfaith Group has shown us something of the richness of the different faith traditions. Each faith tradition has a particular gift for humanity and arguments as to which is the best hinder the sharing of those gifts.

All this raises enormous questions and I was to have a chance to explore them during my time with the South London Industrial Mission. However, that lay in the future, and in the autumn of 1989 I was faced with the prospect of leaving Walsall.

My nine years in Walsall had been such a formative time. Walsall and its people were so much part of me. Those last weeks of goodbyes were both painful and affirming as I discovered how much I meant to the people I had come to love. It was a terrible wrench to leave Walsall, but a readiness to lay down one sphere of work and take on another was part of the life I had accepted when I made my vows. I was in good company. Like many faithful disciples of all faith traditions I was being asked to step out into the unknown, but the welcoming, beckoning God was ahead of me to lead the way into new paths of exploration and discipleship.

South London Industrial Mission

In the summer of 1989 I was asked by the Reverend Mother to move to our Community House in South London. It was my turn to be ready to travel and put all my worldly goods into that one suitcase. I had a problem. They would not go in!

Our vow of poverty requires that we consider nothing as our own. The clothes we wear and the things we use are the property of the community, merely on loan to us and to be treated accordingly. Even living in the convent and working in the local hospital, it was pretty difficult to keep to the one suit-case. I remember one sister in Africa, packing prior to a move, saying with a big sigh, 'For someone who has nothing, I have an awful lot of it!'

There is a definite squirrel tendency amongst many of us. We rarely throw anything away. Envelopes, cardboard, string, plastic bags and many other amazing oddments are kept 'just in case'. Moving at regular intervals does ensure that much of this gets disposed of periodically, or dumped into a communal cupboard.

However, with more varied ministries the goods multiply until, after nine years community work and a theological course, I had acquired a heavy load of books, files, a motorbike, typewriter (later a computer). I did manage to get all my goods into the community car which Gill drove to London while I took the motorbike on the train.

Arriving at Birmingham New Street at 7 am one Saturday morning I rang for assistance and was duly ushered into what seemed like catacombs in order to reach the appropriate plat-form for the London train. One of the lifts was not working so

I really enjoyed riding the bike through the catacombs on to the right platform. It was a great shame that there was no one around at that hour to see a sister in full habit ride up the services ramp on to the platform.

We arrived at Euston about 9 am and I was distinctly nervous of riding through London but it was accomplished without any problems, even negotiating the Elephant and Castle round-abouts, although it was a long time before I plucked up courage to do it again. I was quite terrified by the volume of the London traffic and wondered if I would ever be able to cope. However, the freedom the motorbike gave me was not to be lightly jetti-soned and so after a few very stressful months I became well acclimatized. I even got to the stage of shaking my fist at a taxi driver in Trafalgar Square. 'What's the matter with you?' he growled. 'It's my right of way,' I replied indignantly and rode on. I did later reflect that perhaps I needed to modify my aggres-sion if I wanted to stay alive!

When I came to the London house I was given time to explore and discover what my ministry might be. The old idea of obedience whereby a sister just went where she was told by her superior and undertook any work that needed doing regard-less of her gifts and training has given way to a more open, mutual seeking the guidance of the Holy Spirit. It is now agreed that a particular community work may only continue as long as a particular sister is available. When she moves it is not auto-matically presumed that the sister following her will be able to undertake the same work, an attitude which is both more realistic and effective.

This raises the question of what is vocation and, in the community context, what is a sister's special vocation within the community vocation. I once heard vocation described as something you can't help doing. That effectively describes my entry into the community as a postulant. It was something I had to try, an idea from which I could not get away. Parts of me recoiled from what it involved, especially the clothes and the curtailment of my personal freedom. After I had been fitted for my habit before my clothing as a novice, my novice mistress told me that when it came to the wimple I turned every shade of green. I never grew totally accustomed to it and it was a great relief when a few years later we changed to a simple veil.

The discovery of my particular vocation to interfaith work came much later after twelve years of fitting into other people's expectations of what I should do. I spent those years working in various hospitals which involved some enjoyment and a great deal of struggle, frequent illness, mostly minor but some serious. I accepted it as part of my vocation on one level but on another I felt undervalued, unsatisfied and angry. At the end of the 1970s the writing was on the wall regarding the work of our community in Tanzania. Schools and hospitals were coming under government control. Tanzanians were able to take over from the sisters. The community was not getting new members and the existing members were getting older. We began to see that our life in Tanzania was coming to an end. I experienced some considerable anxiety as I considered what work I might be asked to do in the future. When I expressed this anxiety to the Reverend Mother she said, 'I have been waiting for you to be less busy in the hospital. When you have time I would like us to think and pray together about your future.'

I was amazed by this approach, having been prepared to be told where to go and what to do. I was even more amazed when the time came for us to sit down together. The first question she asked was, 'What do you want to do?' I was so stunned that I had difficulty in answering. Eventually I was able to say that I did not want to go on nursing. I would like to do some form of chaplaincy, perhaps hospital chaplaincy.

I handed my job over to a Tanzanian and returned to England at the end of 1979. It was a crisis point. I had thought in terms of a life vocation in Africa. Now that was over. What did the future hold? It took some considerable time to work through the process of bereavement and cope with the present insecurity. It was a difficult time for the whole community as other sisters were going through similar experiences. There was a great deal of change and inevitably we felt very insecure.

During the summer of 1980, I spent three months doing a

placement in community work under the direction of Canon Sebastian Charles who was then a resident canon at Westminster Abbey. That was a very important time and I valued both his wisdom and the challenge he provided. I had been asked by my community to spend the summer observing aspects of the church work in multiracial areas and he provided me with contacts and introductions which were invaluable and also the space to reflect with him on what I observed. I then had to write a report for the community Greater Chapter at the end of the summer.

Those few months were among the most formative of my life. Early in the placement I said that I thought the community might have a special contribution to make in the multiracial field. Sebastian looked at me rather quizzically. 'Some would say that you are the worst of the lot since you are often so patronizing.'

I duly took note of those words of wisdom. The next couple of months proved to be very challenging. I abandoned my idea of hospital chaplaincy and was eager to get involved in community work. The opportunity came when my community responded to an invitation to open a house in Walsall and I have related some of that story in the preceding chapters. It is a story of a discovery of vocation both for individual sisters and the community in general.

A quotation from Frederick Buechner's book, *Wishful Thinking*, wonderfully expresses the discernment process:

There are all different kinds of voices calling you to do all different kinds of work, and the problem is to find out which is the voice of God, rather than that of society, say, or the superego, or self-interest. By and large, a good rule for finding this out is the following: the kind of work God usually calls you to is the kind of work a) that you most need to do, and b) that the world needs most to have done ... The place God calls you to is the place where your deep gladness and the world's deep hunger meet.[1]

My time in Walsall had been nine years of exploring that process of discernment, a process which was to continue over the next years in South London. For the first three months I explored the locality and visited a variety of organizations in order to discover the local needs and see where I might fit in. I felt that I should put the possibility of interfaith work to one side as it probably was not the issue here. So I did in fact let go in order to concentrate on the new experience and to listen to what God was saying to me in it.

However, my whole way of thinking had changed during my time at Walsall. I was disturbed by the lack of ecumenical activity amongst the churches. The adage 'don't do anything on your own if it can be done together' was in my blood stream. I was also paralysed by much spirituality that was so church-centred and appeared to ignore social and political issues.

After a spell of wilderness experience I came in contact with the South London Industrial Mission. I arranged to have lunch with the senior chaplain, Canon Peter Challen and a very exciting conversation followed. I knew nothing about industrial mission and still had a picture not far removed from that of chaplains going around factories in boiler suits. I was impressed and invigorated by Peter's breadth of vision and enthusiasm. That meeting was like a stream of living water in my dry desert. Peter was excited by my multifaith experience and obviously full of ideas but he did not impose them upon me. He simply said, 'Come along to the AGM and possibly a team meeting and see where you fit in.'

He meant what he said. I am grateful to Peter for many things but what I most value is his ability to say what he means and the enormous trust he has in people. He really does know how to encourage and enable colleagues to make their own unique contribution to the work.

In June 1990 I attended a team meeting of the SLIM chaplains as a guest at Christchurch, Blackfriars. It started with a eucharist at 7.45 am followed by breakfast when I was able to meet all the chaplains. SLIM has for many years been an ecumenical network of Christians committed to exploring the relevance of faith to work. To enable the wide network of associates there was a core team of chaplains, lay and ordained, from most of the main churches in South London. In 1990 there was a very strong team of fourteen members from the Roman Catholic, Anglican, Baptist and United Reformed churches.

At this first team meeting there was news of a conference, 'Three Faiths, One God?', being organized by the Modern Church People's Union. It was to be held at High Leigh and provided an opportunity for Christians to explore their relationship with Judaism and Islam. I was asked by the team if I would be willing to attend that conference as a delegate for SLIM and report back to the team. This I was delighted to do and the subsequent conference for three days in July proved to be a very important experience.

The keynote lectures were by Rabbi Norman Solomon, an Orthodox Jewish scholar at that time from the Jewish/Christian Institute at Selly Oak, Birmingham, Dr M. Mashuq ibn Ally, a Muslim Scholar from St David's University, Lampeter, Wales and Bishop Kenneth Cragg, an eminent Christian scholar who has made an extensive study in Islam as well as working for years in the Middle East. We also had Christian responses from Richard Harries, Bishop of Oxford and Keith Ward, Regius Professor of Divinity at the University of Oxford.

We worked for some time each day in small groups to discuss issues which arose. Apart from the speakers nearly all the conference members were Christians and I found myself rather frustrated since they only seemed to want to look at personal and family issues. Representing SLIM meant that I wanted to discuss issues relating to the workplace and the environment. I came away from the conference thinking that Judaism and Islam had a better theology with which to address political and economic issues. As I reflected I realized that it was only because Christians had lost touch with their roots in Judaism.

After this conference I was even more committed to the wider ecumenism, in fact I was fired by a vision. I had come to see that it is urgent that people of faith work together on the issues which affect the future of our society and planet. In fact, unless we did start to co-operate, I saw serious dangers ahead for us all. I also came to see that Christians must give up attempts at proselytizing, since until we did, people of other faith traditions would not trust us enough to work with us. It is urgent that members of the different faith traditions gain a better understanding of each other and so grow in trust and learn to work together.

This crystallized my thoughts on mission. I am not dispensing with the idea of mission or even proclamation. Christians do have a message to proclaim. The good news of God's total and unconditional love revealed in Jesus Christ is something that the world needs to see even more than hear. Christians have often talked about it too much and not lived it. As John V. Taylor says in his book *The Go-Between God*,[2] 'We have to be the gospel.'

My report to the SLIM team was very well received and subsequent discussion revealed that there was a real desire to explore this further. However no member of the team had any experience of interfaith dialogue and they did not know where to start. At this point I went back to my community and discussed possibilities. It was agreed that I could make an offer to SLIM of the equivalent of two days a week in order to make contact with other faith communities in South London, build up a network of relationships and promote some dialogue on economic issues. This was received by the SLIM team with considerable enthusiasm, the job description and framework for my work clarified and once again it was 'on my bike' to explore.

Although I had found my niche in terms of work with the permission of my community, there were growing difficulties in my life at the Community House in London. I found myself a bit of a 'square peg in a round hole' and for a variety of reasons it was thought best if I moved out and continued my work from a different base. The timetable I was keeping was definitely not 'convent friendly' and there were many tensions which were proving damaging to my health and the peace of the house. My first move was to share a flat in Brixton with a friend who was a Medical Mission Sister (Roman Catholic). I lived with Magda for nine months and this was a great support to me during a difficult transition period. At the end of that time my situation was discussed at the Annual Greater Chapter of my community and I was given a period of detached service for two years. This could subsequently be renewed and was in fact renewed twice while I was working with SLIM.

I joined the congregation of St Matthew's Church, Brixton, which gave me a very supportive base from which to continue the multifaith work. When the Medical Mission Sisters sold their flat I moved into a bedsit in Clapham where my education was advanced enormously, especially through my regular visits to the local laundrette. After three and a half years in Clapham, during which time I still worshipped at St Matthew's Church, Brixton, I moved to 'flat sit' for a friend in Herne Hill for two years. This was a great joy as Mary had a wonderful garden in which I could both sit and potter when I had time. This was a further renewal of my roots, being able to keep in touch with the earth. I found that just to put my hands in the earth to pull up a few weeds revitalized my spirit and centred my being. Eventually Mary sold her flat and I found a basement flat just round the corner. Here I was snug and warm in the winter and able to keep cool from the intense London heat of a hot summer.

11

Being Human Together

I soon found that working in South London was a very different proposition from working in Walsall. Walsall was a smaller area, had a definite identity and people felt that they belonged to Walsall. However, in the South London sprawl there existed many different areas. People lived in one area, worked in another, spent their leisure time and attended their place of worship in others. It was impossible to get a sense of belonging to any particular place in that situation. Borough boundaries were very arbitrary and did not reflect how people related. The minority faith communities came from very wide areas to their places of worship. It was therefore much more difficult to identify local issues of common concern.

There was already a South London Interfaith Group which had recently merged with the Wandsworth and Merton Interfaith Group, and I received an enormous amount of help from the secretaries. I began by exploring existing networks of relationships through such organizations as the South London Interfaith Group and the local branches of the Council for Christians and Jews in Wimbledon and South London.

For the first year I concentrated on visiting places of worship in South London and where I was welcome returning regularly to experience their worship. It did not matter that I could understand very little of the language. I was able to appreciate the atmosphere of worship and prayer, the welcome and hospitality. I knew that it was going to take some considerable time before I could build up the sort of relationships we had in Walsall. Only by spending time regularly could I show that my respect and concern were genuine.

I had met the Revd Tony Crowe, vicar of St Luke's Church, Charlton, at the High Leigh conference, and he was interested and very supportive. He was able to give me the name of the president of a local mosque, Asghar Hamid. He mentioned that he had helped that group of Muslims a few years earlier when they had been trying to buy a local property in the face of considerable local opposition.

I duly turned up on the doorstep of the president's home one Saturday morning. My ring on the doorbell brought a group of small, curious children to open the door a few inches. 'Is your father at home?', I asked. Some of the children disappeared to call him while the others continued to stare at this strangely dressed woman on the doorstep. A few minutes later a rather grim face, viewing me with great suspicion, appeared at the six-inch gap of the doorway. I took a deep breath, knowing I had to get my message over quickly or that door would be closed. I mentioned Tony Crowe's name and at once the atmosphere changed. A broad smile appeared on Mr Hamid's face and the door was opened wide. I explained my wish to arrange a meeting for members of the local church and mosque. That was fine if it was Tony's church and he offered the hospitality of the mosque for a Saturday morning.

A few weeks later eighteen Muslims and Christians met at the mosque to discuss 'What does it mean to be human? How do our faith traditions help us to be human? How can we help each other to be human and work together for a more humane and just society?' Right from the start the atmosphere was cordial. We received a very warm welcome. Tony Crowe was present and I consider that this meeting would not have been possible without his earlier support for the members of this mosque.

We shared our stories of creation and all agreed that being human meant being in relationship with God, our fellow humans and the environment. We found that we had a great deal in common, although there were some sharp differences and some considerable heat was generated when we talked about our different understandings of Jesus. We also found that we had different attitudes to law. The Christian understanding was that God's law has to be interpreted and that the ten commandments were a basis. The Muslim viewpoint put forward was that of the absoluteness of the laws revealed to the prophet Muhammad.

We agreed that it was important to accept and respect our differences while working together on what we had in common. After about two hours of discussion and enjoyment of generous refreshments, it was decided that we should meet again. We planned to meet again at the mosque and the next subject for discussion was proposed by one of the Muslims. 'How can Church and Mosque work together for Peace and Justice?' As the Christians left the Muslims said how grateful they were for our visit. 'We need your co-operation to create social harmony.' Little did we realize how important these meetings would prove to be.

Two months later we met as planned. By this time the Gulf War had been going for ten days. We came together with a sense of enthusiasm and purpose, glad that we had already met and that relationships of trust were already beginning to grow. The subject took on a real sense of urgency. What effect was the Gulf War having upon us locally and what could we do together? The Imam spoke of God's displeasure with good people who do nothing. The Christians saw some comparison with the story of Abraham pleading for the few righteous people in the condemned city of Sodom. They were in danger of destruction since they had done nothing about the evil around them, an evil which many rabbis consider was more about neglect of justice and care for the poor than sexual immorality (Gen. 18. 16–33). It was agreed that we all had a duty to feel from the heart what was wrong, to protest using the power we had ourselves and to approach people we knew with power. It was pointed out by the Muslims that if one Muslim is attacked then all feel it. It was a bit like a family, which normally quarrels, uniting against someone who attacks from outside. Saddam Hussain standing up to American imperialism was like a monster standing up to a bigger monster and something on to which racism could latch. Some thought we were called to repent of a lifestyle which made excessive demands for oil and so aggravated the situation.

After some pretty energetic discussion we decided to draw up a common declaration and send it with an account of the meeting to national, local, church and Muslim newspapers. We wanted it to be known that, while 'Desert Storm' was raging, local Muslims and Christians could sit down together.

An hour and a half's very hard work followed in which we sought to draw up a statement to which we could all assent. The process was probably more important than the product. During the process we learnt so much about each other as a phrase acceptable to the Christians was unacceptable to the Muslims. We discovered that words like judgment and repentance were used differently in the different traditions. Christians wanted to say that we all stood under judgment but that was unacceptable to the Muslims since judgment referred to the Last Judgment. Repentance was also a much stronger word for the Muslims and referred to the need of someone who had fallen away from Islam. Eventually we agreed on this statement.

> We believe in One God, Lord of Creation, God of Justice and Peace, who will judge all people with mercy and compassion. We declare our common concern for the destructive effects of the Gulf War on God's creation and the hatred it can generate among God's people.
> We pray together for a just and peaceful solution.

We prayed together in silence and then the Muslims and Christians prayed in turn. The Imam led the following prayer for the Muslims which was recited in Arabic.

> In the Name of Allah, the Beneficent, the Merciful.
> Praise be to Allah, Lord of the Worlds,
> The Beneficent, the Merciful.
> Master of the Day of Judgment,
> Thee alone we worship; Thee alone we ask for help.
> Show us the straight path,

The path of those whom thou hast favoured;
not the path of those who earn Thine anger nor those who go
astray.

After a short silence the Christians recited the Lord's Prayer
together.

We arranged that the next meeting would be at St Luke's
Church and we took leave of each other with a sense that
something very important had happened. When we next met the
Muslims came with the news that their mosque had been
vandalized. It was thought that it was probably youths who had
broken in one night and damaged the prayer hall, tearing up
copies of the Qur'an and painting the carpet with graffiti. We
were deeply shocked by the news and felt a great sense of outrage at the violation of that holy place. This led us to talk about
the rearing and education of children.

We continued to meet on Saturday mornings about every two
months alternating between mosque and church. Topics for
discussion ranged from Jesus in the Qur'an and Jesus in the
Bible to almsgiving and wealth sharing and what it means to be
a successful human being. We did not really get to grips with the
last one since we had such difficulty in defining what we meant
by successful, although we were pretty much in agreement
against the popular understanding of it meaning fame and material riches.

At one meeting we talked about Hajj, the pilgrimage to
Mecca which all Muslims are expected to undertake once in
their lifetime if their situation permits, that is if they have
adequate health and sufficient wealth. Some Muslims have
undertaken it many times and it can be undertaken on behalf of
someone who is unable to perform it. The Imam had just
returned and so was able to tell us something of the experience.

'Id-Al-Adha', or the Festival of Sacrifice, coincides with the
end of the pilgrimage and commemorates the testing of
Abraham's obedience (Islam) by God in being asked to sacrifice
his son Ishmael. The Qur'an tells how the child was ransomed
and in joyful remembrance of this act of divine mercy, pilgrims

offer the ritual sacrifice of sheep or camels. In the Judaeo/ Christian tradition the son was Isaac. It was interesting that at this meeting we were able to accept that our stories were different without argument as to who was right.

The following December we again met at the mosque and to our dismay found that there had been an arson attack. We were taken upstairs to the prayer hall to see that the pulpit had been pulled down and a fire lit. Everything was blackened and the holy books charred. I cannot begin to describe our feelings of outrage, shame and helplessness at this second attack on the mosque. It was a small and depressed meeting. What could we say to our friends who were so distressed? It was the beginning of the end of our regular meetings. The distress of the Muslim community and serious illness amongst some of the leaders meant that the Muslims did not have the time or energy to continue the meetings.

However the contacts remained and I have a wonderful memory of Tony Crowe's final service in St Luke's Church on his retirement when the Imam recited a blessing from the Qur'an and those beautiful Arabic words echoed round the church. This vividly illustrated the point that the Qur'an is meant to be heard rather than read. It is a spiritual experience just to hear those words, even if you do not understand them.

As I write this six years on I reflect with amusement that I am now described as a regular at the local Hindu temple and at the Gurdwara. I am invited to call in any time at the local mosque and the Rabbi teased me on one of my visits to the synagogue by announcing that he was going to ask me for my membership subscription.

All this is about being, rather than doing. Prayer has been described as wasting time with God and community as wasting time with each other. Developing interfaith relationships requires as much time as it does building any community. I was exploring what Christian mission meant in this diverse multicultural, multifaith world of South London. How was the message of God's total and unconditional love to be proclaimed?

Unconditional love means that we accept people as they are. It means a profound respect for them and their beliefs. It means taking the trouble to try to understand what is important to them, seeing where God is already at work in their lives and being ready to learn more about God from them.

Mission is a word with a bad history. For many people of other faith traditions it has meant lack of respect for all that they hold dear, it has meant a barrage of words and no listening. It has even meant exploitation and oppression. The word needs to be rescued if we are to go on using it. It is interesting that at a time when some Christians are unhappy about the word in a religious context, the business world has taken it over. Most organizations and businesses now have a mission statement that expresses the purpose of their existence. What would be an appropriate mission statement for a church taking seriously the multifaith nature of our world?

I believe that we have to find a common mission before we can effectively proclaim the particular mission of Christianity. The concern of all the great faith traditions is authentic human living, of providing the space and climate for proper human flourishing. It is about enabling people to grow as responsible members of their families, faith communities and society. The Walsall experience shows how people of different faith traditions have many concerns in common. With so many forces at work today which diminish our humanity it is urgent that people of faith work together to overcome them. At a time when there is so much fear and distrust about, building up trust is probably the most important thing we can do. In that atmosphere of trust we can grow in respect for each other and learn to appreciate the richness of each other's traditions.

'True dialogue means sitting alongside the member of another faith, seeking to see through his or her eyes, to understand the riches of the other's religion, and to share, if the other will allow it, in those riches.'[3]

Through 'faith-full' dialogue my hope is that people of faith will be able to lay aside their defensiveness and discover a common mission for the world, the proclamation that God is love and that that love is for everyone without distinction. God is present in his world, already working his purpose out and calls all people to respond, to co-operate, and to share.

12

Rediscovery of Roots

Weekends were the best time for finding places of worship open and people about. Sometimes I could make a phone call in advance and arrange a meeting. At other times this was not possible and I would just take a chance and turn up. I happened to be passing through Streatham one Saturday morning after a visit in that area and thought I would just find the locality of the South London Liberal Synagogue. As I approached I saw the doors were open and people coming out. So parking my bike, and quickly changing from crash helmet to nun's veil, I went up to the door. I received a lovely welcome from a young woman who said, 'You must come in and meet our Rabbi.' I was taken to the office where I was introduced to Rabbi Neil Kraft and as I explained my purpose of encouraging multifaith co-operation, he became very excited and said, 'That's just what I have been preaching about this morning. Come in, it's good to meet you.'

There was not much time to talk then but Neil told me that I was most welcome any time and gave me a copy of the bulletin with the times of the services. That was the beginning of a very enriching experience of friendship. One Saturday I returned for the Sabbath morning service. I had not realized in advance that it was to be a Bar-Mitzvah service and it proved to be a most wonderful introduction to Judaism. There had been no Jewish involvement in the Walsall Interfaith Group because the nearest synagogue had been in Birmingham. My first real encounter with Judaism was a profoundly challenging and disturbing experience. The questions raised by interfaith encounter became much sharper and I discovered how limited my understanding of Judaism had been.

The service was in both Hebrew and English and the prayer book or Siddur provided the English translation beside the Hebrew, so that with the regular announcement of page numbers I was able to keep up. My first impression was the joyfulness of the worship. There was an acknowledgment of human frailty and dependence upon God but the service was devoted to praise and thanksgiving. God was praised for the wonder and beauty of creation, the mystery and gift of life.

After the opening prayers and psalms of praise, the service continued with the Shema and its blessings. The Hebrew word Shema means 'hear' and is the first word of the sentence said by every devout Jew on rising in the morning and before going to rest at night. The congregation all stood for the solemn moment when with one voice they recited, 'Hear, O Israel: the Lord is our God, the Lord is one.' This was followed by the recitation of Deuteronomy 6. 5–9.

Then the congregation sat and there followed what was, for me, one of the most moving parts of the service. The music went into a minor key and the congregation sang, 'Remember all my commandments and do them. So shall you be consecrated to me. I am the Lord your God, who led you out of Egypt to be your God. I am the Lord your God.'

Here I had a sense of God calling us to remember who he is and who we are, of God drawing us back to that sense of unity which comes from a right relationship with him. The Sabbath is a time for that remembering and healing from the fragmentation of our daily lives, of joyful letting go and allowing ourselves to be wrapped in the peace of God.

Evagrius, a Christian scholar in the fourth century, described sin as a 'forgetfulness of God's goodness', and at this point in the service, the music and the words touched both my heart and mind, leading me to experience a joyful repentance and returning to God. A sense of 'Ah Yes', and relaxing into the remembrance of the love of God, allowing God to hug me.

The service continued in praise and thanksgiving to God as Creator, Saviour and Liberator, God as the Rock who has always cared for his people and will continue to do so. Thanksgiving was offered for the gift of the Sabbath, with its joy and peace and the opportunity to enjoy, celebrate and so enhance the quality of life.

After these prayers, the young boy who was celebrating his Bar-Mitzvah came to the lectern to give thanks for his Jewish heritage and to promise to go on studying it in the years ahead. He was then invited to read the portion from the Torah. This can be something of an ordeal for a thirteen-year-old as the Hebrew on the scroll has no vowels marked, but those I have witnessed undertaking this task have always performed it very well, thanks to careful preparation by the Rabbi. There was a great sense of satisfaction amongst the congregation at the completion of the Torah reading, and enormous pride for the parents.

After the Torah reading, the Rabbi prayed a traditional blessing for both the boy and his parents, asking that God would protect the boy, enable him to grow to find favour with God and people and that his parents would be privileged to bring him to the wedding canopy. The parents usually come up to the front to take the scroll out of the Ark and remove the coverings before the reading of the Torah. After the reading, the scroll was held aloft while the congregation stood. The scroll was then dressed again and returned to the Ark. There was a real sense of it being a family and congregational celebration and the parents were congratulated as well as the candidate after the service.

The service continued with the Haftarah reading, which is a reading from the prophets and usually supports the theme of the Torah reading. A sermon by the Rabbi followed this. From this, and the prayers around the Torah reading, I got a sense of delight in Torah. It is God's gift, to be embraced as the way to a healthy lifestyle. Embracing the commandments and teaching of Torah is the way to healing. I realized then that the view I had received from traditional Christian teaching was a grave distortion.

A lot of this distortion comes from translating Torah as Law. This is a narrow and inaccurate translation. 'Teaching' is a nearer translation. Translation is always difficult and many of our misunderstandings in the interfaith experience arise from this. Concepts from one tradition and culture often do not translate and we are left with an approximate attempt which is wide open to distortion. However good a translation, when a word is taken out of its cultural context and put into another, it takes on a different meaning.

The conflicts recorded between Jesus and the religious authorities in the Gospels have given Christians a very distorted view of Judaism. I do not dispute that those conflicts occurred, but the legalism Jesus challenged is present in every faith tradition. Plenty of evidence for this is seen in Christianity. To focus on Judaism as a legalistic religion, to be superseded by Christianity, is to miss the point of Jesus' teaching. He was calling people back to that covenant relationship with God, the steadfastly faithful and merciful God of whom many had lost sight with their obsession for the minutiae of religious observance. This was destructive, not only for the legalists themselves, but also for the ordinary people who were made to feel excluded by their inability to keep the endless list of rules.

This legalism seems to be a hazard of institutional religion and I believe that there is much in our present day religious observance which warrants the same challenge that Jesus presented to the religious leaders of his day.

During the Rabbi's sermon the young boy's gifts were affirmed and thanksgiving made for them. He was encouraged in his new responsibilities and the parents congratulated. In both the Liberal and Reform Jewish tradition, girls may also go through this ceremony. It is then called Bat-Mitzvah, Daughter of the Law. In Orthodox Judaism only boys are called to be Sons of the Law. At thirteen the young person is considered to be old enough to assume the responsibilities of an adult Jew. Liberal Judaism considers that this is too soon so confirmation takes place after the age of sixteen, usually as graduation from religion school. Here the emphasis is on the young people confirming their adherence to Judaism and they take the service. Sometimes young people leaving religion school do not feel ready and so confirm their lives as part of the Jewish community when they are a bit older. I have been present when a young man in his twenties made his confirmation. He led most of the service and gave a very moving address as to why he was choosing to be part of Liberal Judaism.

The service ended with the greeting 'Shabbat Shalom' and this greeting was exchanged amongst the congregation. The translation, 'Sabbath Peace' is totally inadequate. The Sabbath is seen as a foretaste of the messianic age and is a time of great joy and happiness. When the Sabbath lights, the two candles, are lit at sunset each Friday evening, the Sabbath is welcomed as a Bride, as a time of blessing with the message of God's abiding love. It is a time of delight, of enjoyment of family life, when the whole family gathers to share special food.

'Shalom' is a word that has lost much of its meaning when translated into the word 'peace'. The very sound of the word Shalom conveys a more rounded, whole meaning. Shalom means the wholeness of all people and the entire created order. It includes all our relationships, with God, with ourselves, each other and the environment. We cannot begin to understand Judaism unless we recognize the relationship between God's promises and the land. Shalom is God's gift but we have to co-operate with him in bringing about his Shalom.

We then went downstairs to the hall to share Kiddush. Everyone was offered a small glass of wine which was held until the raising of the cup by the Rabbi and the recitation of the blessing by all present. 'We praise you Lord God, King of the universe, Creator of the fruit of the vine.' We then drank our wine.

Then the plaited *cholla* bread was similarly blessed and broken into fragments and distributed. On ordinary days there followed tea and biscuits but on special occasions such as a Bar-Mitzvah, the family provides special refreshments. At this point everyone started chatting and exchanging news. I was made to feel most welcome and many were delighted that I had come.

I came away from my first service at the synagogue with much food for thought. It had completely exploded my former knowledge of Judaism. Here I had experienced 'Creation

Centred' spirituality with a delight in the love and wonder of God in creation and his presence and salvation in history and daily life. There was a sense of wholeness and of being rooted in ordinary human experience. The celebration of the Sabbath gave holiness to the rest of life. Being human was a precious gift of God and everything in the world created for our enjoyment. Jews believe that at the final judgment we will be asked the question, 'How have you enjoyed my creation?'

I came away with a deep sense of Sabbath Peace, a sense of being rooted, of being a creature of the earth, of accepting myself and my circumstances, a sense of God in all things. This sense of at-one-ment had come through the process of re-membering. Through the remembering of who God is and who I am, the scattered fragments of myself were drawn together in a true remembering. I now realize why this is the crucial focus of Christian worship, that we remember who God is and who we are, made in his image and redeemed by his love.

Any ideas that Judaism had been superseded by Christianity were sharply challenged, as was the sweeping judgment that Judaism is legalistic and Christianity is about freedom. I experienced a freedom with the things of the earth and enjoyment of life which can be sadly missing from some Christians. This earthiness with its acceptance of human fragility and mortality, the wholesome sense of humour which accompanies it, has enabled Jewish people to survive the most appalling hardships and persecutions. God's blessings are to be experienced in the here and now and salvation is longed for now!

There is a variety of understandings regarding the figure of a messiah and the messianic age and it has never been as clear or uniform as traditional Christian teaching has suggested. Some Jews do not believe in the coming of a messianic figure but look forward to the messianic age when God's reign on earth will be complete. It is the duty of us all to bring the messianic age nearer by working for a better and more just world. The main reason for Jews not accepting Jesus as the messiah is that the messianic age has clearly not yet come. This has to be taken seriously and is a great challenge to Christian triumphalism. To see the victory of Christ over sin and the coming of God's reign purely in personal and spiritual terms is to fall far short of the radical and dynamic fullness of New Testament teaching.

There is an unfortunate attitude that the Old Testament has been superseded by the New Testament and therefore the former need not be studied. I regret that there are still many churches where the first of the three readings at the Sunday eucharist is omitted. We end up forgetting that Jesus was a devout Jew, misinterpret the teachings of the New Testament and therefore we become out of touch with our roots.

A very healthy movement which is occurring now is this rediscovery of our Christian roots in Judaism. The Council of Christians and Jews over the past fifty years has done much to overcome distortions and misunderstandings between Jew and Christian and so improve relationships. The seminars and courses of Jewish/Christian Bible Study organized by CCJ have been very exciting in opening up a new understanding and love of the scriptures. The Rabbis have a distinctive method which is both intellectually challenging and well earthed in human experience, with a delightful light touch provided by their wonderful sense of humour.

The importance of the recovery of our lost roots is crucial for the development of a holistic theology which will enable Christians to engage creatively with the social and political issues of our day. While working with the South London Industrial Mission, I have become conscious of the lack of support given to Christians in their work life. I experience a deep sense of frustration when many church leaders and politicians talk as if moral values only refer to people's sexual lives. Such pronouncements on moral issues are often used to justify a witch hunt for those who do not fit our narrow views of respectability, who threaten our sense of identity, and to provide a scapegoat to relieve our discomfort.

Moral issues are present-day working conditions, job insecurity, long hours, low pay and unemployment which diminish people's humanity and induce such levels of stress that family life is being jeopardized. It is the idolatry of the so called 'free market' which is threatening the stability of our social structures, not single mothers. These are the moral issues which need to be the focus of a debate by people of all faith traditions and none. It is in this debate, at a local level, a small group of Christians, Muslims and Jews in South London have been engaged over the last few years.

13

Meeting of Two Worlds?

One Saturday when attending the South London Liberal Synagogue, Karen Briscoe, a member of the congregation, approached me after Kiddush. She had heard of the project upon which I was working and wondered if she could be of any help. She became a great support in my work and was a key advisor for the SLIM multifaith project, helping with the consultations. She later became a member of the Board of the South London Industrial Mission, often challenging the Christians' patronizing ways of thinking and working. Karen and I became great friends, discovering that our personal journeys were being enriched by each other. As our friendship grew, we attended a couple of Jewish/Christian Study weekends together and following these experiences Karen expressed a wish to visit a convent.

We both found weekends away rather expensive so the obvious place to visit was the Mother House of my community at Effingham, in Surrey. At this time I was having difficulty with my relationship with the community. Both the lifestyle and interests of the sisters seemed far removed from my life in South London and I was beginning to feel that I no longer really belonged. I visited the convent for community days and chapter meetings and kept in regular contact with the Reverend Mother Gloria, who had lived with me in Walsall. She understood the importance of the interfaith work and was very supportive but I did not feel that I had many sisters behind me. It was more a case of 'Sister Maureen doing her own thing!'

When Vivien was at the convent, she was a wonderful support. Although getting very frail and limited by arthritis and forgetfulness, her mind was fully alert when it came to people and interfaith relations. Vivien's love of people, her great interest in all they did and her gift of friendship was central to her life. She might forget to turn up for prayers in chapel and it was infuriating at Walsall when she was quite capable of disappearing in the opposite direction at the time of Vespers, but she never forgot a person. People came first. How I treasure the memories of Vivien seeking me out, eager to hear all about my interfaith activities. Vivien's friendship kept me going when I felt that my relationship with the community in general was rather tenuous.

At Effingham there is a delightful little guest house next door to the convent with two bedrooms, sitting room and kitchenette. Guests are free to make their own breakfast and then have the main meals with the sisters in the convent refectory. The guest house is very well used, especially by local clergy coming for study or quiet days. I was able to book the guest house for the two of us for a weekend in June 1994. I may have been as nervous as Karen. I did not find visits to the convent easy, in fact I felt more like a fish out of water and wanted to rush back to my London lifestyle as soon as possible.

Karen and I were welcomed by the sight of afternoon tea set out in the sitting room, a meal neither of us normally eats, but it looked so welcoming. We settled down to do justice to the bread and butter, home-made jam and chocolate swiss roll. The guest sister kept popping in to see that we had all we required and when I got slightly irritated by her attentions, Karen said, 'You know, she would make a wonderful Jewish mother!'

Karen's first impression of convent life was the friendliness of the sisters, their welcome and genuine interest in her. She had an expectation that all dressed the same we would behave the same and she delighted in our individuality. Vivien was one of the first sisters to come over to the guest house and she and Karen became friends at once.

Silent meals were a great shock to Karen. She accepted it with good humour but remarked that silent meals were very unJewish. It made me reflect on our attitude to food. There seemed to be the idea around that we were only allowed to take food in order to carry on working for God and that somehow the physical is inferior to the spirit. This is reflected in some of the traditional graces said before and after meals.

'. . . that through this food we may make acceptable sacrifices to Thee.'
'We thank Thee for strength vouchsafed to our bodies. We pray that Thy Holy Spirit may increasingly strengthen and govern our souls.'

Although I find silent meals restful and often a welcome option when having been at close quarters to the sisters for most of the day, I do feel that the celebratory nature of the shared meal is missing. Jesus enjoyed his food and wine and his table talk must have been enjoyable, otherwise he would not have attracted so many people to share it.

As we had arrived on Friday evening we arranged that Karen would celebrate Sabbath evening prayers in the guest house after supper on Friday and Saturday. Eight or nine sisters squeezed into the sitting room and witnessed Karen lighting the candles and sharing Kiddush with the *cholla* bread and wine. She explained the ceremony and then we had a time for questions and discussion. Questions ranged freely over Jewish belief and practice and one minute before the silence bell at 8.30 one sister raised the question of the messiah. The silence took precedence over the messiah so we adjourned until the next evening.

Both evenings were memorable. I particularly love the Havdalah ceremony, traditionally celebrated in the home at sunset each Saturday evening. Havdalah means separation and the ceremony marks the point between the end of Sabbath rest, joy and delight and the beginning of the demands of workday life. It is a short ceremony in which the plaited Havdalah candle is lit and passed to the youngest person present. The following or similar words are said, often in Hebrew.

Time has stood still, but now the Sabbath is ending. Soon everyday life will start again. We feel regret at the transition from rest to toil, from peace to struggle, from holy to mundane. But the resumption of the daily round also raises fresh hope. Perhaps the coming week will bring us nearer to the time of which the Sabbath is a foretaste: when good will triumph over evil, and joy prevail over sorrow; the time when the process of redemption will be complete.

As Karen held up the the cup of wine she said a prayer of thanksgiving for the fruit of the vine by which we celebrate, in hope, the day which the Sabbath anticipates, the day when the joy of Sabbath will fill the hearts of all God's people and endure forever. She then held the spice-box saying these words.

The heightened spiritual awareness which the Sabbath confers is fading now . . . As it does so, let these spices console us. For as their fragrance lingers, so something of the spirit of the Sabbath will remain with us, if we let it, in the week to come.

After the prayer of thanksgiving the spice box was passed round for every one to enjoy the fragrance of the spices.

As the Sabbath ends, we give thanks once more for its blessings. The moment of its passing is bitter-sweet, but we let it go in the sure hope that the Sabbath will punctually return for ever.

The Havdalah candle was then extinguished by pouring a little of the wine on the flame. Then it is customary to wish everyone a good week, and often 'Shavua tov, shavua tov' is sung.

A good week, a week of peace;
May gladness reign and joy increase.[4]

This short ceremony was very moving, giving both a real

sense of the meaning of the Sabbath and the importance of moving on. It is a natural human response to want to cling to what is good and beautiful and we all know how hard it is to come back from a good holiday or retreat to the ordinary work-day world. The Havdalah ceremony provides a ritual to help us make that transition, to let go the joys of Sabbath with gratitude and find courage to face the demands of another week in the sure hope of a return of another Sabbath.

I was conscious of a deep atmosphere of both peace and respect in the room. Karen was plied with more questions as the sisters awoke to the realization that they knew very little about Judaism. One sister looked at Karen with a sense of wonder on her face. 'I have never met a Jew before,' she said softly and I could see that a whole new world was opening up for her.

I gazed round the room at my sisters in awe and delight. Something wonderful was happening. They were beginning to experience something of the richness I had found in my friends of other faiths. Karen was doing what no words of mine could do, she was giving them her own experience of rootedness in the Jewish tradition. Interfaith dialogue is about personal encounter, about the awakening of a sense of wonder before the experience of another person. With this wonder comes an open-ness to listen to the other with a tingling sense of excitement as new horizons appear. Only personal encounter can challenge the deeply-held assumptions and world views which stop this profound openness.

This weekend with Karen at the convent was a watershed in my relationship with my sisters. I began to see them with new eyes, eyes that were beginning to be cleared of the blindness of hurt and misunderstanding. My sisters were beginning to under-stand why the interfaith work was so important and I was beginning to respect and listen to them more deeply.

Karen and I reflected together on convent life. It was so different from our life in South London. The Greater Silence from 8.30 pm and early bedtime did not suit our biological clocks one bit, even less, the early rising in the morning. I adapted more easily than Karen since I had once lived that pattern. Fortunately the guest house allowed space for flexibility and Karen could have her breakfast whenever she wished. The atmosphere of silence and prayer and the quiet routine of the convent day made its mark upon us. We both agreed that it was a challenge to our rather frenetic lifestyle. We began to relax and think more deeply about what we considered important in life and think of ways in which we could hold on to some of that ordered peace when we returned to South London. It was rather like savouring the spices at the end of the Sabbath.

Karen had expressed a wish to talk with as many sisters as possible during the weekend. She was fascinated by convent life and wanted to know what made people join a religious order. The sisters took her at her word and there was a steady stream of sisters coming to the guest house over the weekend. Karen said that she felt like royalty! I think there were many confidences shared, as Karen is a very good listener.

Karen came to some of the Offices or prayers in the chapel although, as I expected, she found this quite difficult. When she was able to relate to something like the psalms she then felt alienated by the Gloria recited at the end. 'Glory be to the Father and to the Son and to the Holy Spirit; as it was in the beginning is now and ever shall be. Amen.'

She attended the parish eucharist on the Sunday morning and before the service began spent some time reading the service booklet. There was a brief explanation giving the origins of the eucharist in the Jewish Passover. Karen looked at me indignantly. 'You have taken something precious to me and made it into something alien.'

There was no answer to that one. Something precious to both of us had been given very different meanings. We could only stay with the pain of that realization. Our friendship was strong enough to hold it but it brought home to me how much that is precious to me is painful and disturbing to my Jewish friends.

I was reminded of an occasion at a mosque when involved in discussion with some very militant young Muslims. One was rather aggressively trying to show me that I was in error and started quoting St John's Gospel to prove his point. He believed that the Advocate promised by Jesus in John 15. 26 was the prophet Mohammed. I was shocked and offended by this and angry at his misuse of the Christian scriptures. I endeavoured to keep cool and merely pointed out that I considered that this attack on my beliefs was unhelpful. I respected him and his beliefs and I hoped he would do the same for me.

It was only when I got home and reflected on this exchange that it suddenly dawned on me how Jews might feel about the way Christians have interpreted the Hebrew scriptures or Old Testament. This raises important questions as to how we approach each other's scriptures and underlines the importance of recognizing the integrity of when and how they were written. If we ignore historical context we risk misunderstanding and distortion and leave the way open for misuse in a way that can be both oppressive and exploitative. As the first Christians were Jews it is understandable and appropriate that the Hebrew scriptures were searched and used to explain the meaning of Jesus and I do not want to undervalue the richness of those much loved passages used at Christmas and Easter. But I do want us to have a greater sensitivity for the Jewish experience and avoid regarding as absolute any interpretation we may have.

That experience in the mosque made me very sensitive to Karen's feelings. After the Sunday eucharist she told me that the most threatening moment for her was the sight of the choir procession walking behind the cross. The symbol which is so precious and central to Christians is one of deep pain and unease to many Jewish people. I have discovered that it is inappropriate to enter a synagogue visibly wearing the large crucifix which is part of my religious habit. It is painful and sobering to consider why this is so and to remember the atrocities which have been perpetuated under the banner of the cross. Such a painful history lies between Jews and Christians. We have to live with the pain of this, without denial or excuse, recognizing that wounds do not heal easily and avoiding shallow attitudes to forgiveness. Only so can Jew and Christian begin to live together into a new future.

There was much that weekend which Karen found strange and even difficult but it was a very helpful and enlightening experience for her, as it was for me. The peace and quiet, the friendliness, kindness and hospitality of the sisters was a very healing experience. Karen delighted in the gifts and individuality of each sister and was concerned that their individuality might be suppressed by the lifestyle. 'If the sisters' individuality does not have room for expression, it will come out in foibles.' Karen's very perceptive remark gave me much food for thought. What does it mean to 'lose oneself in the common life' which is an exhortation in the document 'The Spirit of our Community'?

I have come to see that one cannot make a true gift of oneself until one has found oneself. Many of us have been trying to deny ourselves in an unhealthy way which stunts rather than releases our humanity for creative living. The tension between the needs of each person and the needs of the community is a difficult and often painful one. The only creative way is to live with it openly, to keep asking the questions and never settle for fixed answers. Living with conflict is demanding, the alternative is death-dealing. As another friend said to me, 'If there is no conflict someone is getting away with it all the time.'

I was aware that Karen had taken a great risk in coming to the convent. I do not think it would have been possible without our years of friendship and working together. Being together in the guest house avoided Karen feeling isolated. This weekend did much for us individually and as friends. It did a great deal in raising the awareness of my sisters to interfaith issues in a very gentle non-threatening way and started a healing process in my relationship with my community. It was also a restful weekend in peaceful and pleasant surroundings and Karen has since returned several times. Another weekend is booked as I write this and it is something looked forward to by all of us. I am taking a very dear friend home for the weekend.

14

Economics for People

The moral issues outlined at the end of chapter 12 became the focus for the explorations I undertook for the South London Industrial Mission. I was wonderfully supported by Karen and also Rizwan, a Shia Muslim from Tanzania. Rizwan, born in Dar-es-Salaam, was a link with my time in his country. I enjoyed visiting the Hyderi Islamic Centre where the community was largely from East Africa and there I discovered that I still was able to converse a little in Swahili. The project I was doing for SLIM was partly funded by the Christendom Trust, who requested that a monitoring group be set up to ensure that the project stayed on course. Karen, Rizwan and two SLIM chaplains formed that group and we met on a Sunday afternoon over a cup of tea every three months at the Wholemeal Cafe in Streatham. There dreams were shared and plans made.

After eighteen months of visiting faith communities in South London I made plans with the chaplaincy team for an interfaith consultation on 'How Faith Communities Relate to Local Economic Structures'. It was difficult to find a day which suited everyone. Saturday is a popular day for many people but understandably not acceptable for Jews. We wanted a longer space of time than could be provided by an evening so we settled for a Sunday afternoon in October 1991 at the Industrial Mission headquarters at Christchurch, Blackfriars. We planned to start at midday and have a bring and share vegetarian lunch during the proceedings. Most people encountered difficulty on their journey, whether they came by car or public transport, forcibly underlining a major issue in London. We started the consultation an hour late with the issue of London transport at the top of the agenda.

I had sent invitations to all the main faith communities in South London but we only had eighteen representatives from those I had been able to visit regularly, underlining the importance of visiting and building up relationships. We provided a room for Muslim prayers and arranged our breaks to fit in with Muslim prayer times. I had forgotten to provide a sheet on which the Muslims could pray, so an altar cover was hastily provided, to the great delight of both Muslims and Christians. There was something very special about the sight of the Imam leading his people off for prayers bearing the blue altar cover. It set the tone of the afternoon which was one of profound respect and sensitivity to each other. A minor crisis occurred when I discovered that a Christian had brought a pork pie for lunch and placed it in the middle of the table of food. I was most upset when I saw it since just to have it in the room could deeply offend both Jew and Muslim. It was Rizwan, my Muslim friend, who calmed me down and put it out of sight!

After lunch we had a visual presentation from one of the industrial chaplains on what was meant by local economic structures and then we divided into small groups for the sharing of experiences. Public transport was seen as expensive, unreliable and not geared to the needs of disabled people. Unemployment, housing estate problems, lack of resources at all levels of education were major issues for all those present but by far the most important one was racism and discrimination. Where there was an acute shortage of resources, members of minority groups found themselves seriously disadvantaged. The level of unemployment was greater in their communities and access to the education, training, language and communication skills which would enable them to compete more effectively in the labour market was more difficult.

As we shared these experiences and considered some of the teachings of our respective faith traditions, we became aware of how all our traditions have firm teaching on justice and the importance of the common good. It is a matter of grave concern for all of us when some groups of people are disadvantaged and excluded from taking their full place in society.

Although we only had a short time together, the atmosphere of the afternoon was very encouraging. There was a sense of delight and excitement as we talked together and discovered how much we had in common. Sharing our concerns about our communities and families in South London gave us an awareness of the strength of support we could give each other in just meeting together as people of faith. We came from very different backgrounds, cultures, had different religious stories and language, but we were united by our sense of the divine purpose and the sacredness and gift of life. There was a deep sense of being children of the one God and therefore of having a responsibility both to support each other and work together to try and create a society which reflected the values of the reign of God.

It was clear that people wanted to meet again but it was thought that we might get a better response if we used local community premises. The South London Liberal Synagogue in Streatham offered their hall for the next consultation. This produced a larger number of participants from that area but very few from South East London. This showed us that it is better to concentrate on a smaller area if we want to involve people at grassroots level.

Since racism and religious discrimination were the main issues at the first consultation we decided to concentrate on them in our next consultation, 'Minorities in a Modern World', which took place the following February. This time we started with a shared vegetarian lunch at 1 pm and then worked together from 2 pm to 5 pm. It was an afternoon which generated a great deal of energy. Over thirty people attended, many experiencing themselves as marginal members of their own faith communities. Three speakers shared their experiences, a Muslim man, a Jewish woman and a black Christian clergyman.

We then divided into small groups, taking care that we had representatives from all the faith traditions present in each group. Discussion was often heated as many people from minority groups shared their own experience of racism and discrimination. This was painful listening for the white Christians present who were very much a minority group at this consultation. We saw how important it was to bring out into the open the pain and resentment felt, but equally important not to become paralysed by guilt. We had to own the failures and injustices of the past, then move on to consider the possibility of a new future which we could create together.

A tension was identified between being part of one's own community and mixing with the wider society. It was considered important to be proud of one's identity and faith. Language and cultural practices which were not understood were seen to be a barrier to creative relations between communities and there was a great deal of education needing to be done. Church, mosque and synagogue could provide help with education in communication skills, not only for children but also women who have not been able to come out of their homes through lack of confidence.

Anxiety was expressed over the rise of neo-nazism and the racist right and that the lessons of the past had not been learnt. It was thought that we needed more interfaith meetings which led to joint action which was visible and public. There was a need to assimilate to a degree but also maintain our religious and cultural identity, being open enough to exchange ideas and learn about other faith traditions and cultures. We ran out of time and only just began to share the teachings of our respective faith traditions but a statement by a Jewish person present summed up what many people thought: 'We have a religious obligation to help one another to get along in life.'

The next consultation was held at the English Martyrs church hall, Streatham, in May 1993. This took place at a time when there was a series of meetings in the capital looking at the Health and Wealth of London. It was called 'Healthy, Wealthy and Wise?' and eighteen Jews, Muslims and Christians spent the afternoon looking at what their faith traditions said about the relationship of health and wealth. We again had a speaker from the Muslim, Jewish and Christian traditions, followed by small group discussion. Wealth was seen as far wider than material things. It included the rich human resources we ourselves represented, especially our children. It included our shared experience, wisdom, goodness, abilities and talents. We were all in agreement that everything we had was God given, that we hold it in trust and will be judged both by what we do with it and by what we are.

We considered how we could share the wealth of our community strengths and resources. Racism and discrimination were impoverishing all affected by them. Poverty often did mean poor health, but a so-called high standard of living was often proving unhealthy. Pursuit of wealth can jeopardize the health of the environment and future generations. It was considered that we had a duty to create a more compassionate society and be less egocentric. Again a Jewish comment from the teaching of the Talmud provided a succinct statement: 'We have a duty to "live healthily" and to "repair the fabric of the world".'

'Living healthily?' was clearly a good topic for our next consultation and six months later, in January 1994, we met at the South London Liberal Synagogue to consider how we live in harmony with ourselves, each other and the environment. We followed our usual programme of a shared vegetarian lunch at 1pm, which was proving to be very popular, followed by an afternoon of speakers and discussion. This time we invited Jonathan Gorsky, Education Officer from the Council of Christians and Jews, to speak on the social aspect of living healthily and Musrrat Hussain, Co-ordinator of the Muslim History Group, to speak on our relationship to the environment.

Jonathan gave us a most thought-provoking talk from the perspective of the Orthodox Jewish tradition. He thought that the word 'community' had become a political word without substance. He expressed concern about the signs that we were becoming an uncaring society, in particular, the attitudes to the stranger. He contrasted present day attitudes to biblical teaching: in particular the observance of the Festival of Tabernacles emphasizes the nature of human life. During this festival Jews spend some of their time in an incredibly fragile structure called a 'succah' or booth. They remember how they lived in these fragile structures when they emerged from Egypt. This festival occurs soon after the Jewish New Year, setting the tone for the coming year in which Jews are obliged to share with the poor and lonely. The succah is called a place of wholeness or a place of peace and here people are valued for their essence rather than their possessions.

Jonathan considered materialism to be a spiritual illness and the solution to develop a community where people do not feel that they require material goods in order to be valued. This is also the message of the Sabbath when traditional Jews gather as a family and economic activity is forbidden. Jonathan said, 'The world ceases to be an object of endeavour, we stand aside from our labour and the physical world recovers its sanctity.'

Musrrat Hussain then highlighted aspects of Islamic teaching on the environment. Islam teaches that the environment is God's creation and to protect it is to preserve its value as a sign of the Creator. Environmental ethics are based on the concept that all relationships are based on justice and equity. To presume that the environment is only for the benefit of humans leads to environmental misuse and destruction.

Mohammed said, 'When Doomsday comes, if someone has a palm shoot in his hand he should plant it.' This saying from the Hadith encapsulated the principles of Islamic environmental ethics. Even when hope is lost, planting should continue, for planting itself is good and will continue the process of development and sustain life even if one does not anticipate any benefit.

In the discussions which followed these talks our main concern was what practical action we could take together. We agreed that we needed to encourage a sense of belonging, supporting the family and linking the home, place of worship and school so that we could create a safe environment which would enable children to move out into the world with hope. It was important that the belief that people matter was shown in the way our respective organizations functioned. We needed better education at all levels and to find ways of joint faith community responses. At this point we decided to develop a network of people in touch by telephone who would try to respond to local events and issues in appropriate ways.

The following September we held another consultation at the South London Islamic Centre on 'Faith in Work?' We started with the usual shared lunch. The Muslim community were delighted that we were holding the meeting at their centre and had gone to a lot of trouble to give us a warm and generous welcome. It was therefore disappointing that so few people attended. I experienced a deep sense of frustration as the people who needed to have their negative views of Islam challenged were absent.

After lunch twenty people settled down to discuss attitudes to work and their experience of working conditions. All our faith traditions teach the dignity of work, work as co-operation with God our Creator, work as a means of caring for creation and a way in which we become the people God has created us to be. Work is not just what we are paid to do. So often there is a hierarchy in work reflected in the monetary reward given. Unpopular tasks, essential for health, are often given a very low value. Women's work, especially in the home where it is unpaid, is very under valued. Indeed, if a woman looks after the home and is not in paid employment, she is labelled 'economically inactive'. (I would like to see what would happen to the economy of the country if such 'economically inactive women' were to withdraw their activity for even one day.)

I once asked an economist about this labelling, and he agreed that it was inadequate but that we had to have some way of defining people's activity. Such labelling by those in power reveal a very dubious value system. We need a more humane way of valuing people and a more appropriate way of rewarding work. When so many people are excluded from paid work, particularly young people with little hope of a career, how are they to discover a sense of dignity, self-worth, self-discipline and growth in responsibility to each other, society and the earth?

Participants agreed that for many people work is becoming a

less pleasant experience. There is a loss of confidence and faith in work itself. Many people are increasingly stressed in their work and this is having an adverse effect on family relationships and the atmosphere in which the next generation is growing up. A large number of people in their early forties are considering early retirement. They would rather settle for a simpler lifestyle. Quality of life is not about a high standard of living. Many people doubted that we are better off than we were thirty years ago. There are pressures in society which push us into a false view of the human person. Capitalism feeds on greed and envy and this is reinforced by our advertising system.

Our religious traditions teach us that the value of a person does not depend on achievement, property or physical appearance and ability. The human person is not just a consumer or a factor of production. In the present economic system workers are regarded as costs rather than assets. All this has a very dehumanizing effect upon people and undermines their sense of self-worth which can only have a detrimental effect on society. Economics is for people, not people for economics!

At the end of the afternoon it was decided that we would send the following letter to the Secretary of State for Employment expressing our concerns.

Dear Minister

As representatives of different faith traditions in South London we the undersigned met at the South London Islamic Centre on Sunday 25 September 1994 to discuss the relevance of faith to present day working conditions. At this meeting several concerns were expressed.

Many people are experiencing levels of insecurity and stress at work which are reducing their effectiveness, jeopardizing their health and placing great strain upon relationships at work and at home. This in turn is having an adverse effect upon the environment in which the next generation of 'wealth creators' is growing up.

If human resources are treated as mere factors of production and basic human needs are ignored, people will be unable to make their full contribution to the economy of this country. We wish to point out that an unhappy work force is uneconomic.

It is important when quoting scripture to use it in context. 'Whoever refuses to work is not allowed to eat,' comes in Paul's rebuke to those who were ignoring their responsibilities because they expected the imminent return of Jesus Christ. Such teaching should always be read alongside such passages as I Corinthians 12 verses 24–26 which teach the responsibility of a community towards its weaker and disadvantaged members. 'If one part of the body suffers, then all the other parts suffer with it.'

We are deeply concerned both at the number of people who are excluded from employment and those in low paid work which denies them adequate human living, a sense of self-worth and opportunity to make a meaningful contribution to society. We consider that society is judged by its treatment of the disadvantaged and less privileged. As a society which has its roots in the Christian tradition and which in many areas still claims to be Christian we would suggest a closer attention to our responsibilities towards these people. We also believe that a denial of their opportunity to contribute fully to society is flawed in economic terms.

We, as members of different faith communities in South London, would like to express our concern at the effect the rising level of stress and insecurity of those people in paid employment is having upon their quality of life. In both the short term and long term this is uneconomic.

That letter, signed by Muslims, Jews and Christians, represented a very important process in our journey together.

15

One World, Many Faiths?

The experience of the consultations, together with my personal contacts in the course of visiting places of work and worship, confirmed my belief that economics is an important area for interfaith dialogue. It is a key area which affects the lives of us all, whatever our race, colour or creed. Yet I found that most people have difficulty in engaging in discussion about economics because they frequently feel deskilled by the language used. I struggled myself to understand economic theory and language and in the process woke up to the realization that there is a mystique surrounding economics. It stops people asking awkward questions and that is exactly what is wanted by those whose interests are best served by the existing system.

Economics, like theology, is defined by those in power and who have most to lose by a challenge to the system. Theology and economics both tend to be in the hands of experts, usually white, male and western. Any new theories usually have to be measured against certain givens. These givens are extremely powerful, have their own language and concepts which perpetuate the mystique which discourages questioning. Both disciplines tend to develop theories apart from every day life. Economists who label housewives as 'economically inactive' probably know little about what goes on in the kitchen. Theologians living in academia have little understanding of the experience of the presence or absence of God in the everyday pressures and challenges of life. Yet it is the theory of these so-called experts, both in economics and theology, which shapes our lives and even more powerfully, shapes our thinking.

The word economics comes from two Greek words, *oikos*

meaning house and *nomos* meaning law or management. So economics is simply about the management of the household. In Hebrew understanding the world is God's household.

> How precious is your steadfast love, O God!
> All people may take refuge in the shadow of your wings.
> They feast on the abundance of your house,
> and you give them drink from the river of your delights.
> For with you is the fountain of life;
> and in your light we see light (Ps. 36.7–9).

Economics is about how we organize the management of our life together on planet earth and therefore we all have both a real interest and an expertise in such economics.

Ecumenism is another important word and has generally been restricted to meaning co-operation between different Christian churches. Yet the word comes from the Greek word *oikoumene* meaning the one inhabited earth and it is to this level of dialogue that the South London Industrial Mission is committed. There is only one race and that is the human race. The most important thing about us, what ever our belief system, is that we are human and as humans we inhabit one earth. The Chief Rabbi, Jonathan Sacks, has said so very succinctly: 'God has created many universes of faith but only one world in which to live.'

We are all faced today by a world crisis as to how we live together and share the resources of this one earth. Economics as the management of God's household and the exercise of our stewardship as trustees is the concern of all people of faith. As human beings, supported by the earth's wonderful but fragile ecosystem and as people of faith with a sense of the giftedness of life and our responsibility to cherish it, we have an urgent common agenda.

Unfortunately, all too often, the dogmas and claims of religious traditions are put before this common agenda and are used to increase, fuel and even legitimize our human divisions. Religious claims have been used to uphold lust for power and an unjust hold on the earth's resources. Religion has been, and still is, both blessing and bane in the world's history. People of faith urgently need to discover ways of working together towards a more just, participative and sustainable way of living together on this planet.

With such a massive agenda it is easy to feel overwhelmed by the enormity of the task and be paralysed by guilt. Therefore we need to consider what we can do on a local level within our own neighbourhood. As a Christian I follow Jesus Christ, who declared that he had come to bring fullness of life to all. I do not believe that the life he offers is for our souls only. The abundant life which he brings is for the whole person and that means the physical, mental, social, political and economic aspects of our lives.

Our discipleship has to be within the area of our everyday life and relationships. It is about quality of life, about how we go about the very ordinary humdrum events of our lives. Gloria, with whom I lived in Walsall, put her finger on it when she tried to describe our Sikh friend, Dilbagh Mavi (see chapter 7). 'There was something very special about him. He had a quiet, spiritual dignity and there was something distinctive about his eyes; something which could not be put into words but which was there whatever he was talking about, be it the weather or his work at school.'

Dilbagh's faith shone out of him. It was an unselfconscious expression of his view of life, the fruit of his deep contemplative life of regular meditation and worship. He was certainly always ready to give an account of his faith and what motivated his life but the power of his witness lay in who he was. Sadly, about a year after I left Walsall, I received the news that Dilbagh had died suddenly at the age of fifty-six years. Two thousand people attended his funeral which was a mark of the esteem in which he was held. It was a devastating loss for all who knew him.

In our series of interfaith consultations in South London we found that the things which united us were greater than the things which separated us. We all had a deep concern about the sort of society in which our children were growing up, about their education and prospects for employment. There was a great concern about employment conditions, job insecurity and the environment. A frequent question was, 'In what sort of world do we want our grandchildren to grow up?'

This is a key question because it challenges short-term policies and makes us consider the sort of world such policies are creating for future generations. As people of faith we all shared a sense of being stewards of God's gift of creation with the obligation to pass it on to future generations enhanced rather than despoiled.

I said earlier that it is easy to be paralysed by guilt when facing these issues. Guilt is a very poor motivator. Melvyn Matthews, in his wonderful book *Delighting in God*, points out that it is delight which creatively motivates us to change.

> Delight is life lived as gift. The discovery of life as a given experience is a discovery of God. Delight stems from the acceptance of what is, as good, and the thankful abandonment of any striving for identity. Delight then releases energy: energy to create, to overcome evil and to defeat disaster.[5]

It is the vision that we are created for delight by a loving Creator who passionately desires our happiness, which liberates the energy to creatively work for change. A great deal of energy was apparent at our consultations. We enjoyed meeting together and deep friendships were formed. The energy came from the delight we found in each other's uniqueness and our differences became the distinguishing marks of those for whom we had a great respect and affection. We no longer wanted to change each other, rather we wanted to listen and receive the richness of each person. We began to appreciate the particular difficulties which each faith community encountered and a strong determination to support and help each other developed. Our determination to resist every form of racism and discrimination came from the delight we had in each other's uniqueness. A multiracial, multicultural, multifaith society was an enrichment not a threat.

My experience as an industrial chaplain with a growing

concern for dehumanizing working conditions and injustice in society and my life of prayer within a religious community opened me up to both the glory and tragedy of life. There were such glorious possibilities and great wisdom in our respective faith traditions about ways of living together in society and caring for the environment. We all had a sense of being called to something greater and wanted to reach out to a better future. Yet we were all faced with the gap between the wisdom and the practice. How could we help each other to be more in touch with the wisdom and to bridge the gap between that and our practice?

In October 1993 the Inner Cities Religious Council (ICRC), a government initiative under the Department of the Environment, held a day conference at Blackheath in South London. The purpose was to bring together members of faith communities and government departments to facilitate joint action for change in inner city and deprived areas. Representatives from the faith communities in South London had been invited and we spent a lot of the day in borough groups sharing our concerns. There was considerable ambivalence about this government initiative, but most of us decided to use the opportunity provided to develop further co-operation between faith communities.

Follow up meetings were arranged in each inner South London borough and the Lambeth representatives met the following month at the Ahl ul Bayt Islamic Centre in Clapham. Many of us had met before, and those of us currently involved in the consultations sponsored by the South London Industrial Mission saw an opportunity for the practical response for which we had been looking.

So the Lambeth MultiFaith Action Group came into being. It was a rather grand title for a very modest group but we wanted to concentrate on action together. The Group was made up of representatives from the Orthodox and Liberal Jewish communities, the Sunni and Shia Muslim communities, the Bahai community and a broad spectrum of Christian churches in Lambeth.

We met every two months, taking it in turns to host the meetings at our respective places of worship. This gave us a chance to learn more about each other's customs and practices. The meetings became a source of delight and inspiration as our understanding and respect for each other grew and friendships deepened. We shared light refreshments before the meetings and a highlight of our meetings at the Ahl ul Bayt Islamic Centre was the strong Arabian coffee served by Jaffar. We were able to give each other support both in the personal events and stresses of our own lives as well as the community issues.

During the first few meetings, we discussed our priorities and agreed our aims and objectives. These were, to explore areas for action in Lambeth to counteract racism and religious discrimination and to promote better understanding between local communities with joint action where possible or desirable. A variety of ideas were shared and we had to decide on more modest projects which stood a chance of being carried through. We were all busy people and did not have great resources, although the most valuable resource was there, the enthusiasm and will to work together. The South London Industrial Mission generously allowed us stationery and the use of the photocopier. We passed the hat round when we needed funds for postage and other expenses.

The telephone network, set up after one of the consultations sponsored by SLIM, was developed and we found this a very valuable resource on several occasions. The Ahl ul Bayt Islamic Centre was plagued by repeated vandalism and 'break ins'. The Liberal Synagogue had several unpleasant experiences, including antisemitic graffiti on the doors and a brick thrown through the window. Following these attacks, a small group of Muslims and Christians attended the synagogue for Friday evening Sabbath prayers to express concern and support for the Jewish community. However little we could do, these small acts made a lot of difference for communities who felt very much under threat. We also sent a joint letter to the local press deploring such attacks. We wanted to say, as loudly and clearly as possible, with one voice, that we were opposed to racism and religious discrimination of any kind and regarded the cultural, racial and religious mix in society something to be valued and cherished rather than feared.

As members of the Lambeth MultiFaith Action Group, we were discovering the enrichment brought by our friendships. We were also conscious of the destructive effects of ignorance and prejudice which hindered the sharing of that richness and made members of minority groups unwelcome and disadvantaged. We were determined to counteract this by putting on a programme of education and celebration for people in Lambeth.

Celebration is crucial. Any programme of education must be enjoyable, an invitation to come and see the richness and fun of a multiracial, multifaith gathering. Again there was the problem of finding a time and day which suited everyone and we found that Sunday afternoon seemed to be the best time. We started at 1 pm with a bring and share vegetarian lunch and this again proved to be very popular. We then had a programme from 2 pm to 5 pm which gave people time to be free for evening engagements.

Table fellowship was central to the ministry of Jesus, the welcome and enjoyment of all who wanted to share. The shared meal was a time for sharing our humanity, of sharing who we were and delighting in the distinctiveness of each other. This sharing deepened friendships and awareness of the various dietary laws made us more respectful of and sensitive to each other. The bring and share meal was full of exciting discoveries as we sampled unfamiliar dishes and enjoyed the exploration of what was new. This sort of meal is sacramental of our life together, discovering and delighting in each other. For me it is a wonderful celebration of the God I worship, God as Trinity, Unity in diversity; the generous, prodigal God who delights to dance through the glorious diversity of creation and invites us to dance too.

One of the highlights of the past few years has been our One World Week Celebrations, evenings of shared food and entertainment. They have mostly been held at the South London

Liberal Synagogue where the hospitality of the Jewish community has been wonderful. We usually followed the theme of One
World Week such as 'Living on the Edge' and 'People on the
Move'. The different faith communities provided material for
exhibition, showing how they were affected by the issues
reflected in the theme of the week.

We circulated posters a couple of months before the event,
inviting people to volunteer their talents for the shared entertainment. I found that few people volunteered and there were
always anxious moments before the evening. People were better
at volunteering each other, which meant tactful and cajoling
telephone calls on my part. However, it was fine on the night
and I learnt just to let things happen and take the risk (a lot
of people were sharing it with me). The informality and spontaneity of the occasions increased our enjoyment. We always had
additions to the programme on the night, particularly when it
came to story-telling. Everyone loves a story and people can
produce wonderful things when they relax.

We had solo singing and a choir, humorous monologues and
a magician who was a great success and we were very sorry
when he moved away from the area. One year I led some
simple circle dancing illustrating our desire to move along
together. That was not acceptable to the Muslims, who sat out
of that activity. Many Muslims are not happy even to be present
at such activities, so shared entertainment has its problems.

One year we included slides of Shia Holy places and that
glimpse of a wonderful tradition, largely unknown in the West,
was most moving. I longed for more people to know about this
tradition so a few months later we arranged an evening in St
Leonard's church hall for a slide show and talk on the Shia
tradition in Islam by some members of the Hyderi Islamic
Centre. Then people were invited to attend the Ashura procession and celebrations which were due to take place in a few
weeks time.

Those One World Week celebrations were very special. They
took on the atmosphere of large family gatherings or reunions,
a family which was always open to new members.

16

Celebrating Our Identity

Several important festivals are celebrated during spring and early summer, Passover for the Jews, Easter for the Christians and Baisakhi for the Sikhs. The dating of all Islamic festivals is dependent upon the sighting of the new moon since the Islamic calendar is lunar. Therefore the festivals are not fixed to any one season but rotate through all seasons. In 1997 Ashura, a central festival for Shia Muslims, was celebrated in May. Sharing these celebrations led me to reflect on the importance of celebrating our community stories. That year, renewed by the Christian observance of Holy Week and Easter with its strengthening sense of identity and commitment to discipleship, it was a delight to observe other groups celebrating their identity.

The Sikh festival of Baisakhi falls on 13 April and is the most important day in the Sikh calender. Baisakhi was an ancient and popular north Indian festival but has taken on a new meaning for Sikhs. It now signifies the birthday of the Khalsa (the pure ones). The birth of a distinct people came about on Baisakhi Day 1699. On that day the Guru Gobind Singh, the tenth Guru, summoned his followers and put them to a severe test. 80,000 Sikhs gathered at Anadpur (City of Joy) to celebrate the festival and receive the 'darshan' or blessing. Guru Gobind Singh appeared with his naked sword in his right hand and called out for an exceptional sacrifice. He asked for five volunteers prepared to offer their heads as sacrifice for the religious cause. Although dismayed by the demand, five men stepped forward and they were taken to a nearby tent to be sacrificed.

Not long after, to the wonder of the thousands gathered there, Guru Gobind Singh emerged, followed by the five men garbed in flowing saffron robes. They were then baptized by the Guru, anointed and given Holy Amrit to sip. Amrit, the nectar of life, is sweetened water, stirred by an iron double-edged Khanda (dagger) in an iron bowl, while five selected passages from the Guru Granth Sahib are recited. The five were then called 'Panj Piare' or the Five Beloved Ones. Sikhs were given a new slogan, 'Sat Sri Akal' (Truth is God) and a new greeting, 'WaheGuru Ji Ka Khalsa, WaheGuru Ji Ki Fateh' (Hail God's Khalsa, Victory is God's).

After this, Guru Gobind Singh was baptized in the same way by the Five Beloved Ones. Through this baptism the three qualities of humility, devotion and steel-like strength were given. The Guru then ordained the five symbols, the Kekaars or five Ks. They are the Kesh (uncut hair), the Kangha (wooden comb), Kachha (pair of underpants), Kara (an iron bangle) and Kirpan (a sword).

Guru Gobind Singh also gave the name of Singh, meaning lion, to all male Sikhs and Kaur or princess to the women. So Sikhs now see themselves as members of the unique fraternity which lays the foundation of a casteless society, believing in One God, equality of humankind, faith in the Guru's Word and love for all.[6]

At my local Gurdwara, the Tooting Khalsa Centre, Baisakhi is celebrated on the Sunday nearest 13 April. Continuous reading of the Holy Book, the Guru Granth Sahib, takes place during the forty-eight hours before the festival. I arrived at the Tooting Khalsa Centre at about 10.30 am as the congregation was beginning to assemble outside in the courtyard. It was a beautiful, sunny day and the bright clothes of the women and the men's turbans provided a riot of colour, vividly expressing the excitement and joy of the occasion. Children ran in and out of the assembled crowd and clamoured to hold the balloons from the bunches which arrived early in the ceremony.

At about 10.45 am a procession came out of the Gurdwara led by a woman carrying the new flag. She was followed by five men in full ceremonial dress bearing large curved swords. Young men with drums and a harmonium and women with tambourines led the singing of hymns. After a while the tempo increased and two men climbed a ladder in order to take down the old flag which was on the roof at the front of the building. The flag and pole were then laid on trestles, the old flag removed and the long metal pole bearing the Sikh insignia washed in milk and water, mostly by the women. This was an activity obviously held to be an honour and many pressed forward to take part.

When the pole had been cleaned to everyone's satisfaction, the new flag, Nishan Sahib, was brought forward to the accompaniment of loud drumming. At this point the men came forward to help put the new flag on the pole. It had an orange pennant with the Sikh insignia in blue at the top and orange cloth covered the whole of the long pole. When all was ready the flag was raised to shouts of 'WaheGuru Ji Ka Khalsa. WaheGuru Ji Ki Fateh' (Hail God's Khalsa. Victory is God's.)

The joy of the community was infectious as the flagpole was carried up the ladder and put back in place. At this point the balloons were released and dozens of white, blue, orange and yellow balloons, bearing the name 'Khalsa Centre, Tooting', soared up into the clear blue sky. The sense of excitement and community unity was intense at this point and all stood before the flag for prayers led by the priest. This was followed by the singing of more hymns accompanied by the drums, tambourines and harmonium. Kraah Prashaad was then distributed and then everyone went back inside the building for refreshments and the service of thanksgiving in the Gurdwara.

I enjoyed the tasty snacks, sweets and hot cup of tea in the dining room and had a chance to ask questions and talk with a Sikh friend. I learnt that families take it in turns to provide the new flag and it is considered a great honour to do this. On discussing the significance of the colours, I heard that the idea of orange as a holy colour originally came from the practice of dipping the robes of the monks or holy people in turmeric as it was considered to be an insect repellent.

After the refreshments I removed my shoes and entered the

Gurdwara where the service was taking place. This took the usual form of hymns accompanied by drums and harmonium with commentaries and teaching, finishing with prayers led by the priest and a reading from the Guru Granth Sahib. At the end of the service Kraah Prashaad was again distributed as a sign that no one goes away from the Guru without a blessing.

By this time it was about 1.30 pm and time for lunch. The shared meal or Langar is a very important part of the festivities, where all eat together. In the dining room we all enjoyed a variety of curries and chapatis, followed by milk pudding with nuts and spices, and sweets. There were several hundred people to feed but it all went so smoothly. Disposable trays and spoons reduced the amount of washing up, but nevertheless many people had been busy all weekend preparing the food. The tasks are usually divided by the women preparing the food and the men serving it. It is considered to be a great honour to provide the food and there never seems to be a shortage of volunteers or a shortage of food. Second helpings of curry and chapatis were brought round several times.

Sikh hospitality is a wonderful thing. I was made so welcome and I got the sense that my friends were delighted to see me. It was such a joyful occasion in which the Sikh community renewed their sense of identity by celebrating their corporate story. I believe that it is this security in their own identity which gives them the openness to welcome others with different stories. As one woman said to me during the service, 'The teaching is the same.' That is certainly true about ethical conduct and I saw that the celebration of the community story releases energy to live out those ideals.

Just over a month later, on 16 May 1997, I took part in a very different celebration. The Shia community at the Hyderi Islamic Centre, Streatham, was celebrating Ashura. Ashura in Arabic refers to the number ten and it was on the tenth day of the month of Muharram, the first month of the Islamic calendar, that Imam Hussayn, grandson of the Prophet Muhammad, was martyred at Karbala by the banks of the river Euphrates in Iraq. The massacre, which included his family and loyal supporters, has left a profound mark upon the Shia community.

Soon after the death of the Prophet Muhammad, corruption started to spoil the Islamic society which he had created. The rise of the Ummayyad dynasty influenced the style of leadership which came to reflect the tastes of the royal courts of Rome and Persia rather than the simplicity and piety stressed by Islam. The situation worsened when the second Ummayyad Caliph, Yazid, came to power. Aspiring to be the undisputed ruler of Muslims, Yazid tried to obtain the allegiance of Imam Hussayn. When Hussayn refused to submit Yazid ordered his execution.

On learning this Hussayn left Medina for Mecca with his family and companions, hoping that his enemies would not dare to shed blood in that holy place. Yazid sent assassins in the guise of pilgrims to kill Hussayn even if he were found in the precincts of the Sacred Mosque. To avoid sacrilege Imam Hussayn decided to go to Kufa, a city in southern Iraq from which he had received many pledges of support.

By the time Hussayn and his companions had undertaken the arduous journey in the desert and reached the vicinity of Kufa it had come under the rule of a tyrannical governor and the inhabitants of Kufa were too afraid to support Hussayn openly. Yazid had dispatched his army to find Hussayn and communicated with the governor to stop Hussayn in the desert.

So Hussayn with his family and loyal companions were forced to pitch their tents in the desert sands of Karbala. They arrived at Karbala on the second day of the month. Over the next few days the army of Yazid gathered in thousands to intimidate Hussayn and force him to give his allegiance to Yazid. This Hussayn refused and on the seventh day the water supply was blocked off by the army. For three days the Imam and his companions suffered thirst in the hot desert until the fateful day of Ashura.

After explaining to his enemies why he refused to submit to Yazid, the Imam and his seventy-two companions confronted the army of thousands. Despite three days of thirst and the heat of the desert they fought bravely before being martyred. Shia

Muslims see this as a battle between faith and purity of thought and action on the one hand and depravity, greed and material power on the other. After the slaughter the camp of the Imam was ransacked and the remaining women and children taken to Damascus where they were humiliated and imprisoned in degrading conditions. It is recorded that the sight of the caravan of captives on the way from Kufa to Damascus and the descriptions of the battle at Karbala stirred the feelings of the Muslims and rekindled their faith. Soon after the tragedy, different movements arose within Muslim society, to protest at the unjust killings at Karbala and at the degrading manner in which the pure descendants of the Prophet had been treated.[7]

I was invited to join the procession commemorating this event on the first evening of the festival. The sombre tone of the celebration was emphasized by the weather. The sky threatened a storm as we started and soon we were walking in the midst of a thunderstorm. The inclement conditions made no difference to the proceedings and added to the effect of the teaching being relayed over loudspeakers. About two hundred Shia Muslims, dressed in black processed through the streets near Streatham Common, the women walking together behind the men. An illuminated model of the tomb of Imam Hussayn was carried by young men and there were many banners proclaiming the central teaching of Islam and quotations of Imam Hussayn. 'To die with dignity is better than a life of servitude.'

I was welcomed to walk with the women and wondered what my blue cagoule looked like amongst all the black robes and veils. My black veil was firmly under the protection of a blue hood. I saw one umbrella, but mostly the pouring rain was ignored or endured in silence. Loudspeakers from a van proclaimed the teachings of Imam Hussayn and the significance of the occasion. Several times we paused for prayers and many Muslims were using the strings of beads upon which they recited the names of Allah. There were so many resonances with the devotion of the Stations of the Cross and the use of the Rosary. I could not hear or understand all that was being said but I was able to pick up the atmosphere of intense devotion and be deeply moved by it. After about an hour we returned to the mosque dripping wet but undiminished in ardour. I was glad to peel off my wet cagoule and shoes and enter the beautifully warm women's prayer room, where we slowly dried out with fans dispersing the moisture-laden atmosphere.

The carpeted floor was laid out ready for evening prayers with long strips of white cloth on which were placed white wraps, beads and small stones. I later learnt that the stones were made from the earth of Karbala which is regarded as sacred and called 'Khak-ush-Shifa'a' meaning 'the Healing Earth'; for it was on this earth that the sacred blood of Hussayn was spilt. Sitting on the floor we first listened to an address relayed from the men's prayer room. This was in English and I listened to the story of Karbala and how the martyrdom of Hussayn is a gift for all people, whatever their creed. The message of the evening was that suffering comes to us all and will often increase if we are struggling in the way of truth and justice. Suffering bravely borne can awake others to a new consciousness and so improve society. The sufferings of those martyred at Karbala were graphically described, which stirred considerable emotion and tears amongst the congregation.

Prayers followed and the women wrapped themselves in the white drapes so that only their hands and part of their faces showed. They got in line, shoulder to shoulder and performed the evening prayer with its familiar prostrations. In the court-yard behind the mosque, models of the events of Ashura were set out in graphic detail with sand, tin soldiers and red ink. I was told that at the end of the ceremonies the following day, the river would be filled with red ink to indicate the day of Ashura, the day of sacrifice and martyrdom.

The prayers continued all night but I left at about 10 pm. Reflecting on all I had seen and feeling the emotion associated with this celebration, I was reminded of the Christian observance of Holy Week with the commemoration of the Last Supper, washing of the feet, the watch in the Garden of Gethsemane, the Stations of the Cross and Easter Garden and I understood the importance of reliving our stories. It strengthens a sense of identity and bonds the community, it confirms ideals and the determination to live them, releasing energy for renewed vision and discipleship.

17

Celebrating Diversity

One of the highlights of my time in London has been the Multifaith Pilgrimage for Peace, organized annually by the Westminster Interfaith Programme which is sponsored by the Roman Catholic Diocese of London. Each year a variety of faith communities have been visited, involving a walk together through the streets of London of anything from six to ten miles on a Saturday in June.

The twelfth annual Multifaith Pilgrimage took place on 7 June 1997, starting on the Isle of Dogs, East London. About fifty of us assembled at Christchurch at 9 am for prayers. After a cup of tea we set off, walking through the foot tunnel to Greenwich. We were a very mixed bunch of people from all over London, the home counties and even some who had come from Oxford and Birmingham for the day. The group also included theological students from Germany who had come to the UK for ten days to look at ecumenical relations. Many nationalities and religions were represented even by those resident in London, vividly showing the rich, multiracial nature of British society.

The procession was led by a Buddhist monk of Nipponzan Myohoji who encouraged us on by the rhythmic beating of his drum. It was a very picturesque party with the different religious robes, the saffron robes of Buddhist monks and nuns and white robes of novices, white robes of the Brahma Kumari and blue of Roman Catholic and Anglican nuns. There were some clergy in clerical dress and others in casual dress. A great variety of clothing was worn by those not in holy orders, some wearing saris or shalwar kameez, others in T-shirts sporting a variety of slogans. Part of the fun of the occasion was talking to as many people as possible on the way between visits and discovering where they came from and hearing their particular concerns. There was a great deal of sharing addresses, literature and giving of contacts to those with special interests.

All were people of strong views with a message to proclaim. A variety of placards were carried to show to the often slightly bemused onlooker what we were doing and why. Several placards advertised that we were London People of Faith for Peace. Others gave quotations from different scriptures.

'Every being is an abode of God, worthy of respect and reverence.'   *Hindu scriptures*

'Let me think goodness, speak goodness and do goodness. Let me hunger and thirst after goodness.'
                                   Zoroastrian scriptures

'Of all the shrines, the most sacred shrine is the heart where the Lord indwelleth.'   *Sikh scriptures*

'Love your enemies and do good to those who hate you.'
                                   Christian scriptures

Having walked through the tunnel, early arrivals, anticipating much footwork ahead, filled the lift to capacity, while others waited for the next shift and the stalwarts climbed the stairs. Once out in the open, south of the river, we walked past the Cutty Sark and into the precincts of St Alphage's Church, Greenwich, where fruit juice and chocolate biscuits awaited us. We had not walked far but talking is such thirsty work! I had been walking with some of the German students and learning about their programme of studies. Then we passed through the picturesque part of Greenwich and up the hill to the railway station. Here we boarded the train to Plumstead, where we started walking in earnest.

Our numbers had swelled to about a hundred by the time we arrived at the Greenwich Hindu Mandir. Here we were offered tea, fruit juice, biscuits and a lovely selection of spicy snacks. As I set out to do justice to the generous hospitality I heard the words, 'Didn't you have time for breakfast, Sister?' 'Yes,' I replied, 'but it was a long time ago!'

My questioner was the local Roman Catholic priest who was interested to know where I came from and the order to which I belonged. Our conversation was cut short by an invitation to join the rest of the pilgrims, now assembled in the prayer hall. The hall was absolutely packed as a large number of the Hindu community were there to welcome us. The place was a riot of colour with the statues of Rama and Sita and Laxman, Krishna and Radha on the platform under brightly-coloured canopies, decorated with flowers and with offerings of fruit and flowers in front of the statues. With the colourful array of costume amongst the Hindu community and the pilgrims it was a real representation of 'God's rainbow people'.

The atmosphere was so welcoming and joyful and full of eager anticipation. The Hindu community was delighted to be part of the pilgrimage and proud to share some of their history, beliefs and practice. The secretary greeted us with a little bow and the word 'Namaste', explaining that it meant 'I honour you because I see the Divine in you.'

We were given a brief introduction to their story and community activities. They believe that God is one and that he shows himself on earth whenever there is a special need, hence the stories of Rama and Sita and Krishna. Hindus believe that God can manifest himself in any creature and this was shown in the variety of pictures around the hall.

We were then led in the singing of a Hindu prayer 'Jyoti se Jyoti jalate chalo'. A translation of this song was given.

Keep the river of love flowing, keep the river of love flowing.
When you come across stray travellers, embrace them with
  love.
Like the light.

Who could be higher or lower if the same God dwells in each
   of us.
It is we who have devised these delusions of rank.
Keep the flag of righteousness flying, keep the river of love
   flowing.
Like the light.
Each particle of this universe is illuminated by the light of
   immortal soul.
There is only one absolute truth and that is; there is only one
   God.
Therefore seek to unify all souls, keep the river of love
   flowing.
Like the light.

Arti was then celebrated, which is a service of light performed
every day at morning, midday and evening. A seven-wick oil
lamp is waved before the statues and bells rung as the prayers
are recited. The prayers finish with the chanting of,

   'Om, Shanti, Shanti Shanti.'   (Om, Peace, Peace, Peace.)

These words now so familiar to me, since I have attended many
such services of worship, have a profound effect upon me. Om
is untranslatable and is the name for the ultimate being
Westerners call God. It is recited with the emphasis on the 'm'
so that it echoes and reverberates in the silence as it is chanted
in meditation.

   The chant was particularly poignant for me on that visit,
since in my annual retreat earlier that year, in the wilds of the
Clynn Peninsula in North Wales, I had become aware of God's
'Yes' sounding through all creation and through my own
history, a wonderful experience of affirmation and love. In an
experience too deep for words I had spontaneously found
myself reciting 'Om' and felt my tiny but glad response of
love and worship mingling with the divine affirmation of all
things. Through this I had been brought to a deep sense of self-
acceptance, wholeness and peace and it was this experience
which was renewed for me when hearing that familiar chant.

The oil lamp was then brought round to the congregation for each person to receive the divine light by the placing of the hands over the light and then passing the hands over the head or touching the eyes. Again I find this symbolic act profoundly moving as it deepens my desire to be filled with the divine light I receive through Christ. 'May the light of Christ fill my mind, purify my eyes and penetrate my whole being.'

The procession then moved on through the streets of Plumstead to the New Testament Church Of God. It was now midday, the day was warming up and the pilgrims filled the church. It was good to get a seat and just sit quietly until we were all settled and ready for the Pastor to tell us about the beliefs and practice of his church. The Woolwich church is part of an international organization operating in 114 countries with the headquarters in Cleveland, USA. The church was founded in 1886 with the aim of preaching the good news of salvation to humankind, irrespective of colour, creed or nationality and the Woolwich church has existed since the late 1960s.

It was good to have members of this church with us and I enjoyed several conversations with the Pastor as he continued with us to the end of the pilgrimage. I found him very welcoming, alight with the conviction of his faith which he was eager to share but also very open and ready to listen, observe and respect those who were different. I sat with him at supper in the Gurdwara at the end of the day after experiencing Sikh worship and hospitality, and it was obviously having a profound effect upon him. It is human encounters such as this which will promote better understanding and so lead to harmony and peace.

We then had a break for lunch which was generously provided by members of the Spiritual Mission of Sachkhand Nanak Dham, an international society whose UK headquarters are in Handsworth, Birmingham. The society was established by Mahraz Darshan Das in New Delhi, India, in 1977, to serve humankind. The society teaches non-violence, vegetarianism, abstinence from alcohol and drugs and exists to promote the love of peace and harmony. A prayer was said before lunch was served which is said by members before every activity: 'Nanak Naam Chardi Kala Tere Bhane Sarbat Da Bhala' (O God, through Nanak, may your Name be exalted, and through your Grace, let there be good done to everyone).

After very satisfying refreshments and many more conversations with friends old and new, we set out again to walk to St Patrick's Church, Plumstead. One of the wonderful things about this pilgrimage is that one meets friends made on previous pilgrimages and exchanges news of the intervening months and shares how far cherished hopes and dreams have progressed. I have found it quite challenging to be reminded of what I shared on previous occasions and stirred to consider how close am I living to my deepest desires?

The large Catholic church is only a hundred years old although the parish has existed for a thousand years. It was wonderful to walk into the cool tranquil atmosphere and just sit in silence as we waited for all the pilgrims to be seated. By this time we must have numbered at least 150 and it was taking quite a time for such a number to move from place to place. We were given a very entertaining presentation on the beliefs of the community and a very warm welcome by its members.

We then walked to the Greenwich Islamic Centre which had been recently built and which can accommodate 1500 men and as many women. We were offered welcome refreshments as we arrived and assembled in the hall on the ground floor to hear a very helpful talk on the beliefs and practice of Islam. Here the usual question and answer time became rather heated when a discussion arose about Jesus as the Son of God. We stayed for some time in the hall while small groups were taken in turn upstairs into the mosque. We removed our shoes and appreciated the beautiful thick carpet under our feet. The simplicity and silence of the mosque was impressive and we walked around with a growing sense of reverence and openness to the integrity of our hosts. There was a sense of being on holy ground.

We then walked to the Woolwich Town Hall where we met the Mayor and Mayoress who continued with us on the pilgrimage to the Ramgarhia Association Gurdwara on Mason's Hill. By this time it was after 6 pm and we were glad to sit in the hall where we were given welcome fruit juice and listened to welcomes and speeches by the Gurdwara committee. It was the eve of the commemoration of the Martyrdom of the fifth Guru, Guru Arjan, and the continuous reading of the Holy Book, the Guru Granth Sahib, was about to start. This would continue for forty-eight hours and then the festival would be celebrated.

After the speeches we went upstairs into the Gurdwara to experience Sikh worship. The priest was praying as we entered and the men stood on one side and the women on the other. The Gurdwara was packed and only a few pilgrims could actually get into the prayer hall. At the end of the prayers the priest started the reading of the Holy Book which would then continue through the night with different members taking turns.

We returned downstairs for a wonderful supper of curry and chapati. There was such a generous supply and second helpings were offered. We numbered about one hundred and together with the Sikh community there was a very large number to feed. However the Sikh community were well used to feeding such large numbers.

As the pilgrims dispersed after supper there was a sense of sadness as we said goodbye to friends for at least another year and returned to take up our everyday lives again. The experience of unity and celebration had touched us all and given us a vision of what life could be like if we could be more open to receive from those who are different. The richness of our multi-faith, multiracial world had excited us all and we had witnessed very powerfully to those who had seen us processing through streets crowded with Saturday shoppers. Delight energized us to return to work and struggle in our own particular situations for a more just and tolerant society.

18

Friendships Renewed

In February 1998 I returned to Walsall for a week in order to visit the friends about whom I have written. It was a time of great joy and encouragement. Sadly the Walsall Interfaith Group no longer met since several key members had moved away and there was no one able to be convener and secretary. Such groups often have a limited life since they depend upon a core of very committed members. However, the work which had been done had not been wasted and many of the friendships formed continued on an informal basis.

I spent an afternoon with Ethel Hinton, now living alone following the death of her brother, Stan. She told of how wonderful her Muslim neighbours had been and their concern that she was living alone. During Stan's illness Sargid and Ajaz had visited him regularly in hospital and the morning after his death they came round to see Ethel. Every evening for two months Ajaz called round to check that Ethel was all right or telephoned if he was very late back from work. Imam Saeed was away at the time but when he returned he and Shabbir visited Ethel to express their condolences. 'If there is anything we can do, please let us know. We are here to help.'

The kitchen window of Ethel's next door neighbours' house faces her kitchen window and Ethel will never draw her blind down while their kitchen light is on. They often wave to each other when in their respective kitchens. Stan had been very fond of the children and there is a real sense that Ethel is not alone, she is part of the extended family. This was voiced by one of the children. 'Aren't you lonely, all on your own? I already have two grandmothers, but I would like to have you as my third!'

Shabbir Hussain invited me to visit his family one morning. It was a wonderful reunion. His daughter Fazia was living nearby, married with a child aged two years. It was so good to talk with her again although I was sad to see her troubled with arthritis in her hands. The Imam, Saeed ur Rahman, also called and there was such a sense of joy in our being together again. Shabbir's wife was busily preparing lunch for us and Imam Saeed suggested that Ethel Hinton be invited also. She was not at home but a note was hopefully put through her letter box. Imam Saeed told me what a wonderful community-minded person Ethel is, how much the Muslim community appreciate her and how concerned they are that she is all on her own.

Shabbir and Fazia showed me round the new mosque which had not been completed when I left Walsall in 1989. It is a beautiful building, spacious with such a prayerful, peaceful atmosphere. I remembered how cramped their old building had been and how very cold it had been during winter. I was delighted at the lovely building they now have and rejoiced with them in their achievement. This achievement is very significant, not only for the well-being of the Muslim community but the wider community also, since society is enriched and made more stable when particular communities have the resources they need for the education and nurture of their members.

The community centre and library are still being built and I was interested at Fazia's comment on the translation beneath the Arabic inscription on the outer wall. 'There is no God but Allah and Mohammed is his messenger,' should read 'There is no god but God . . .' since Allah is simply Arabic for God. I know this to be so since Palestinian Christians call God, Allah.

Our conversations ranged over family and personal news, local news and wider issues, particularly the threat of war with Iraq. Shabbir considered that Sadaam is not 'one of us' and 'he is a very evil man' but did not think that sanctions should continue since they were hurting the ordinary people, they were not hurting Sadaam. However Shabbir was more concerned with what was happening in the Sudan and asked why the West was hindering development there. I had to admit my ignorance of the situation since there is little in the news about the Sudan. I did express my concern about the stories of the persecution of Christians there, about which Shabbir knew nothing. I was left feeling that all the news we get is selective and wondering how can one get at the real truth of things.

Ethel arrived as we started lunch. It was a wonderful meal of spicy meats and salad, with 'the yoghurt to cool the tongue', as Imam Saeed put it. It was a celebration of our years of friendship and all we had shared together, of our shared humanity and desire to serve God. I experienced a great sense of delight and wonder at the way we could meet again and felt myself energized by all those shared memories. It was one of those golden occasions when one marvels at the gift of life and is just so glad to be human. It was with sadness that we parted, hoping it would not be too long before we met again. I left Ethel talking with Shabbir while his son drove me to my next visit. I had a strong sense that Ethel was in very good hands and that she was going to be given companionship and support by the Muslim community.

I had earlier contacted the family of the late Dilbagh Singh Mavi to obtain permission for the publication of my comments about him. Their response, as with the Muslim community, was that I did not need their permission since I was free to write about my own experience. I was invited to tea by the younger son, Kam Mavi, who was living with his wife and two children and Dilbagh's widow in the house I had visited so many times. It was a very emotional occasion for me, and probably for us all, as I sat in a familiar chair talking with the family, overlooked by a magnificent photograph of Dilbagh. He was sitting cross-legged in front of the large picture of Guru Nanak in the sitting room with a radiant smile on his face. The photograph had managed to capture the light in his eyes. The photograph was taken a few months before his death and I could not help feeling that Dilbagh had known that his time was short. This was borne out by Kam relating how his father had advised his elder brother, Jagdev, during those last few months; the significance of this was only realized by the two brothers after their father's death.

Kam, who had been twenty-six years old when his father died, spoke frankly about his deep sense of loss and feeling too young to assume such responsibilities as came his way. He longed for his father to advise him and asked me how one could know that one is achieving the right things in life, how can one measure progress. I was impressed by his depth of thought and quality of questions and struggled to put into words my vision of what it means to be a responsible human being. My words were about openness, a readiness to learn, compassion, concern for justice and other people's well-being and a readiness to forgive. I shared St Teresa of Avila's teaching that a prompt and ready forgiveness is the test of real prayer. We talked of how difficult that is but agreed that we could not make progress as human beings without it. We are closest to God when we forgive.

These are the things which encapsulate human progress and any sort of career or economic activity is necessary to support our families and enable these human qualities to flourish. We talked about vocation and the different functions and roles within society. In seeking to choose the right course in life I shared my experience of the Ignatian discernment of spirits as tools for life and that I considered it more appropriate to find a wise person who would help one to ask the right questions rather than give answers. There is a great danger of abdicating responsibility if we seek out someone who will tell us what to do. We agreed that our religious institutions contain too many people who want to be told what to do and this gives an unhealthy amount of power to the priesthood or leadership.

Kam's elder daughter, Preeti, aged six years, proudly showed me how she could recite the Lord's Prayer and we reflected on how that is a universal prayer, since there is nothing in it which cannot be prayed by people of most religious traditions. After providing me with a delicious tea, Kam asked me if I would say a prayer for the family. I said a short prayer finishing with these words based on the Aaronic blessing in Numbers 6. 24–26.

May the Lord bless them and keep them; may the Lord make his face to shine upon them and be gracious to them; may the Lord lift up the light of his countenance upon them, and give them peace.

Then Preeti said, 'When we pray at school we always say the Lord's Prayer.' So I asked her if she would like to say it, which she did with great competence. Then I asked the family if they would like to recite the prayer in Punjabi which occupies a comparable position in their tradition and which every child learns at an early age. The translation of this prayer has been given in chapter 8 but I understand that it cannot adequately be translated. It is as well that we realize that translation always loses something, since it means the transference of ideas into another culture and thought form. I love to allow those words in Punjabi to float over me and feel the spirit of praise and adoration which no translation can adequately convey.

My heart was full as I said goodbye to these friends. It was difficult to converse with Dilbagh's widow owing to the language difficulty but as I exchanged the traditional greeting of placing our cheeks side by side I said quite spontaneously. 'Your husband meant so much to me.' As she wept on my shoulder I felt the pain of her deep sense of loss. Such a wonderful man had gone from amongst us, a terrible loss to his family and the local community. I shed my own tears and knew the reality of a language which crossed all barriers of language and religion.

The next day was Sunday and Kam collected me in his car and took me to the Guru Nanak Sikh Temple in Caldmore for evening prayers at 6 pm. The particular form of this act of worship is not one I have experienced in other Gurdwaras. I removed my shoes and went upstairs into the prayer hall and approached the platform which held the Guru Granth Sahib before which I made the customary bow of respect. As I turned to take my place amongst the women I caught sight of my dear friend Bhajan Singh standing at the back of the hall. I was overjoyed to see him looking so well, radiant in fact. The last time I had seen him was a few months after the death of his close friend, Dilbagh Mavi, when he was grieving deeply. Now there was a new light in his face and a deep centredness about his person. He later told me that Dilbagh had guided him to another saint who would now guide him on his journey. We exchanged the traditional greeting of hands together and a little bow, then we clasped each others' hands in delight at meeting again. We sat together at the back of the hall for a short time before Bhajan said that he had to go forward to help lead the prayers.

The service had started with a reading from the Guru Granth Sahib and the recitation of prayers by the priest. Then about ten men sat in front of three microphones and started to chant prayers. The main Sikh prayer which I have quoted before was recited by the whole congregation for about fifteen minutes. Then followed the repetition of the words 'Wahe Guru' as a mantra for another fifteen minutes. Since this is addressing God and the closest translation in English is 'Wonderful Teacher', I had no difficulty about joining in with the chant. As I let go and relaxed into the rhythm of the chant I experienced a sense of centring down into communion with God and solidarity with this worshipping community. The next chant was Guru Gobind Singh's prayer which continued for a similar period of time.

Then we all stood as the priest stood in front of the Holy Book and recited prayers. This finished with the congregation prostrating and the responses, 'WaheGuru Ji Ka Khalsa, WaheGuru Ji Ki Fateh' (Hail God's Khalsa, Victory is God's).

Then the priest returned to reading at random a passage from the Guru Granth Sahib before the Holy Book was wrapped in beautiful clothes and carried in procession to the Sachkhand and laid to rest for the night. The service ended with the usual distribution of Kraah Prashaad described in chapter 3.

Notices were given out by a member of the committee and Bhajan Singh came forward to give me special words of welcome. I then followed the congregation downstairs where we all had Langar together. I was able to meet old friends and Bhajan Singh told me how much I was missed in Walsall. I reflected, probably not as much as I miss the people of Walsall. This was my last evening and the next day I had to return to the convent in Surrey.

That evening I realized how much I need my friends of other faith traditions. For me the experience reflects something of the rich diversity in God's creation and that unity in diversity is part of the nature of God. I am excited and challenged by being confronted with other world views; they push me beyond my boundaries and help me to sustain an openness and readiness to learn, giving me an awareness that my perception is limited and there is something new to discover every day.

My interfaith experience has taught me that life is about dialogue. The quality of attention I have learnt to give to my interfaith friends, trying to resist the temptation to push the experiences into mental boxes, has given me a greater openness in other parts of my life. I have discovered the gift of wonder which enables me to stand before another person with awe. This has been particularly helpful in my community relationships. It is so easy to take the people we live with for granted and think that we know them. This attitude stunts both our growth and that of others. Each person is a mystery. I am a mystery, and it will take more than our lifetime to explore that mystery. Wonder or awe is the beginning of Wisdom (Ps. 111. 10).

Wonder nourishes a tenderness and respect that enables us to really listen, to pay attention, to step gently lest we tread on someone's dreams. It opens us up to new ways of seeing, drawing us on to ever greater attention and therefore fresh discoveries of God at work in the world.

I was at a meeting of the Council for Christians and Jews in London when a Rabbi was leading us in a Bible study. We were looking at the story where Moses asks, as a confirmation of God's favour, to see God's glory. God grants him this favour but says that Moses cannot see God's face because no one can see that and live. So God puts Moses in the cleft of the rock and shields him until God's glory has passed by. Then God's hand is removed and Moses is allowed to see God's back (Ex. 33. 17–23).

It came to me so clearly then that we cannot see God directly but we can see where God has been. My experience of God in prayer is mostly that of darkness and silence, but I see signs of God's presence in everyday life. I can see where God has been and that sums up my experience of these interfaith encounters.

19

Discerning the Spirits

A friend reading the previous chapters asked me why I was still a Christian. That very important question seems a good focus for this chapter. Through the rich and varied experiences of my interfaith encounters my humanity and experience of God have been enriched. I believe that I have grown as a human being and have become more deeply rooted in the experience of Christ.

There is a very powerful image in Psalm 1 of the righteous person as a tree planted near water, able to withstand heat and drought. Only with strong roots in the firm ground of my faith in Christ, nourished by that water of life, can I live with the ambiguities and contradictions of the interfaith experience (Jer. 17. 7–8).

It is not just my personal experience of Christ but the corporate experience of the faith community to which I belong. However ambivalent I may feel about the Christian church at times, I still recognize it as the bearer of the Jesus story, and that corporate experience has held me through all the questioning and perplexity of my interfaith journey. That journey has not been without the pain of doubt and confusion, and I have been tempted to try and make it all fit in a dry intellectualism. However I found that this did damage to the richness of all the faith traditions, stunted my own Christian growth and blocked the streams of my creativity.

It was my encounter with Ignatian spirituality which gave me the tools with which to work through my difficulties. It has been said that the greatest gift which Ignatius Loyola gave to the church has been the rules for the discernment of spirits. In the light of my Industrial Mission experience, I would want to add, it was his gift to the world. I have discovered that those rules or guidelines, freed from ecclesiastical language, have illuminated many conversations in the workplace.

My first encounter with Ignatian spirituality came through an eight-day individually guided retreat at St Beuno's Retreat Centre in North Wales. I went there because I was becoming increasingly dissatisfied with preached retreats. I soon discovered why. Here I was given the space to explore my own experience, and listen to what God was saying to me through the scriptures, under the guidance of a Roman Catholic sister. I was no longer having to listen to the experience of male priests who preached at my community retreats and so I discovered and owned my own experience as a woman, learning to rejoice in its distinctiveness. That experience of liberation made me realize how differently people can view things, according to their history, culture, gender and personality. To allow one group to dominate, formulate theology, religious discipline and practice is a powerful form of oppression and control. It influences the thought-patterns and self-understanding of all other groups. Minority groups are forced to define themselves in the terms of the dominant group.

What is true for the woman or the black person is also true for people of faith traditions other than Christian. It is urgent that those of us who are white and Christian in Britain take time to try and hear the experience of people from those other traditions. We will never understand fully, there will always be contradictions and ambiguities because we will always have our different thought-patterns and world-views. The Christianity which has dominated so much of the world has a Western dress. Even when the outward expressions are made indigenous, the theology and ways of thinking are frequently eurocentric. There is notable work being done by theologians from countries outside Europe but too few of us in the West are reading their work.

I eventually did the full Spiritual Exercises in a thirty-day retreat at St Beuno's, although I was called out of retreat at the end of the third week because my father was dying. The two

days and nights at my father's bedside, his death and the subsequent bereavement all became part of the experience of those
Exercises. The experience did not fully flower until five years
later; by then I realized that I had tools for life. The Exercises
are said to be descriptive rather than prescriptive. I discovered
that they reflected the pattern in my life, of death and resurrection, of repentance and renewal, of both delight and darkness,
and a deepening sense of the call to follow Christ and share his
mission to proclaim the reign of God.

The Spiritual Exercises are structured around meditation on
the life, death and resurrection of Jesus Christ and it is this
encounter with Christ at the heart of the Exercises which has
given me the sense of firm roots and of a well within, bubbling
up and energizing my life. The imaginative contemplation of the
Gospel stories has given a sense of the reality of the person of
Jesus; not a concept as in the days of my dry intellectualism,
but a living presence. In retreat I am able to pray in a way not
usually possible in daily life especially when I am tired, but the
retreat experiences have given me a foundation on which to rest
at other times.

In my community we have one day each month in retreat, a
welcome space in a busy life, often just to flop before the Lord.
It was on one such day in Easter week a few years ago that I was
feeling tired and low, a failure as a human being as well as in
my work. I was nourished and upheld by the pattern of a daily
eucharist even though I felt I was not really in it. Good Friday
had been so real, Easter had not yet come in my experience. The
day before my retreat, my attention was gripped by the sentence
at the end of the Emmaus story which had been the Gospel
reading at the eucharist that day.

The Lord has arisen indeed, and he has appeared to Simon!
(Luke 24. 34).

Those words took hold of me and I decided to meditate upon
them during my retreat. In prayer I imagined how it might have
been for Peter, crushed by his sense of failure, and identified
deeply with that feeling. In my imaginative prayer I saw Jesus

come in to Peter, place his hand on Peter's arm and call his name. Peter was still unable to look up, so Jesus put his finger under Peter's chin and lifted it up until Peter's eyes met those of Jesus.

Then quite spontaneously, I was aware of Jesus doing just that to me. I felt the warmth of his hand on my arm and then his finger under my chin and for a split second I had an inner picture of his eyes looking into mine – a gaze of such utter love and delight, compassion and understanding. That gaze of love penetrated my whole being. When I became aware of myself again I was weeping. I felt an incredible sense of being understood and accepted, of being able to relax and accept myself. It was a moment of melting, of letting go so much of my fear and defensiveness. I was unbelievably loved. It was not a love which makes the best of a bad job, but a love of delight and enjoyment.

It was that moment which crystallized and confirmed my picture of Jesus in the Gospels which had been motivating my approach to people of other faith traditions. From praying the Gospel stories I had discovered a Jesus who delighted in creation and the rhythms and patterns of life, who loved, welcomed and enjoyed people. Jesus showed a welcoming, hospitable, inclusive God who welcomes all, especially the social outcast and the sinner; a God who has a special care for the marginalized and the poor, who even seems to have a preference for such people as those who know their need and are open to receive.

Jesus was constantly crossing boundaries, so declaring every person of importance to God. He did not cross those boundaries in order to change people, he proclaimed by his presence the Kingdom of God and left them to respond in their own authentic way. He did not tell people what to do. He told stories which highlighted basic principles of the life of that Kingdom, leaving them to work out the implications. He did not demand an acceptance of a belief system; the Gentiles who came to him received the answers to their requests without a demand to change their belief system. An example is the centurion who came in faith asking Jesus to heal his slave (Luke 7. 9).

The faith Jesus commended was an expectation and openness to let God work, an openness to accept the unexpected. The devout religious people who had a tight belief system measured all they encountered by their perspective. Consequently they were blinded to any new experience which did not fit their narrow world-view. Their closed minds prevented them from seeing the possibilities of the Kingdom. Is that the state which Jesus called sin against the Holy Spirit; to be so sure one is right that one cannot see the presence of God in what is strange and unexpected?

This does not mean that discernment is unimportant. It would be foolish to suggest that everything that is new and strange is good and from God. Here I have found the Ignatian discernment of spirits so valuable. It has helped to assess the value of interfaith experiences. I make no claim for the following to be a definitive account of the Ignatian rules for discernment of spirits; rather it is the way I have adapted those rules to illuminate what is happening in my life. Basically I ask myself:

What is creative and life-giving in my life, leading to an increase in faith, hope and love? What energizes and makes me feel most truly myself, making me more sensitive and aware of other people's needs and more open to respond in concrete compassion? What causes my humanity to flourish in joy, purposefulness, gentleness and truth and justice?

What is destructive and death-dealing in my life, leading to a loss of hope and energy? What clouds the vision and blocks the streams of joy and compassion, causing me to be turned in on myself and indifferent about truth and justice?

These questions have to be asked of the corporate experience too. What makes a group more hopeful, rejoicing in God, at peace with each other and more open to accept and co-operate with those outside the group? What motivates greater compassion, tolerance and service both within and outside the group?

What makes a group fearful, withdrawn, introspective, and concerned only with its own survival and therefore defensive and suspicious of those who are different? What leads to arrogance and bigotry? If a belief system justifies these things then we have to question whether it is of God.

I am aware of the danger of seeking an easy, safe peace. That too seems to be a particular temptation of religious people. Religion can be used in so many different ways, both to avoid conflict and to fuel it. Always the peace which is of God is founded on truth and justice. I am therefore unhappy about any interpretation of Jesus which reinforces defensiveness and intolerance, which divides people into them and us.

To interpret Jesus' words in John 14. 6, 'I am the way, and the truth, and the life. No one comes to the Father except through me' in a way which excludes people who are not Christians (or Christians like me!) runs entirely counter to the whole life and teaching of Jesus. In the light of all that Jesus stands for, I believe we can only interpret that statement inclusively. The difficulty is changing a mind set which has been fixed on an exclusive interpretation. This statement comes in response to Thomas' request to be told the way to God. It comes as a reassurance along with Jesus' declaration of the width of God's welcome and mercy in the many mansions (John 14. 2).

No part of St John's Gospel should be interpreted independently of the prologue (John 1. 1–14). The Word or Logos was seen as the all pervasive spirit of the universe, the spirit of love, and the writer of St John's Gospel was at pains to show that Jesus Christ is that Logos.

The claim in John 14 is that the Logos, the all-pervasive Spirit of the universe has come to earth in Jesus. It is the Logos who is the way, the truth and the life, spoken in Jesus Christ. Christians understand Jesus to be God's fullest expression of his Word but we can never limit God by saying exclusively so.

> . . . the Eternal Word is not a cult-object in the possession of the churches nor an esoteric device traded by mystagogues. It is the creative voice that speaks by means of anything or everything which impinges upon us in the ordinary business of our daily lives.[8]

I have discovered the Word of God coming to me in such varied and unexpected ways over the years of my multifaith work. The Word comes to me in both delight and challenge. That creative voice sometimes encourages and confirms my path, at other times pulls me up hard and causes me to rethink the way I am going. On the occasions I have related in earlier chapters, I have seen the fruit of the Spirit in the courteous welcome I have received when entering a place of worship, in the kindness and generosity of the hospitality and the commitment to the good of both the faith community and the wider community. God is to be found where there is commitment to justice and better community relations.

I have recently experienced in a very concrete way the reality of belonging to a particular faith community and to a wider community of faith beyond the boundaries of the particular. I suddenly lost much of the sight of one eye and found myself unable to read or drive. I was told there was no treatment. My life came to a standstill. It was a terrible shock. I had to cancel engagements. I then discovered more deeply what it meant to be supported by a community of faith. The care and offers of help were overwhelming. I was prayed for by so many people of different faith traditions.

Gradually I adjusted to my new situation, the unaffected eye strengthened and I began to pick up the threads of my life again. However something had changed. I had discovered a strength in being vulnerable. In facing the possibility of not being able to do so much, I entered into a deeper quality of being, and that quality of being was about relationships. It was a concrete experience of the reality that faith knows no boundaries. It was an awesome and humbling experience to be prayed for by so many people and something for which I am profoundly grateful. God comforted and strengthened me through my own faith community and through my Muslim, Jewish and Sikh friends and through them God gave me healing and new life.

Jesus gave a yardstick for discerning true from false prophets, those who speak God's word and those who do not, in Matthew 7. 15-20. This yardstick can be used to assess both our actions and our beliefs. If our religious belief makes us narrow and defensive, arrogant and bigoted, sure that we are right and others wrong, then I think we need to question where such a belief system comes from. 'Thus you will know them by their fruits' (Matt 7. 20).

We are called to be fully human and Jesus showed us what that means. It is not about political and economic success. It is about vulnerability and frequent failure, about an undefensive openness to life as it is, about compassion, self-giving and service without ulterior motives.

It is this vulnerability which is at the heart of the Christian faith, not an imperialism which seeks to dominate and turn others into people like us. It is about not only a willingness, but a positive encouragement, to let others be different, be themselves, be the people God has created them to be. Here the image of God as Trinity is such an inspiration and encouragement. God as 'giving life, bearing pain and making whole' in a great dance of delight and letting be.[9]

The bronze sculpture by David Wynne of the Tresco children in the Scilly Isles is a wonderful image of that delight and letting be. Three children are playing, the older boy holds a younger boy high in the air supported and encouraged by a girl. 'Freedom, trust, encouragement, mutual support and enjoyment in relationship' are the words of a friend responding to that joyful image.

That is the inspiration for my vision of God as Trinity, of community living and all human relationships. We are put on this earth for joy and delight. How can we work together to make that true for those around us, especially the poor and marginalized in our society?

20

Towards a Faith for the Millennium?

When I consider the experiences of the past eighteen years and the journey which the story of this book spans, I am filled with wonder and gratitude. I am conscious that I have grown as a human being and as a Christian and that that growth has been nourished by the encounters with friends of many faith traditions. The journey has not been without its pain, and many times I have felt way out of my depth, but the belief that faith is about living with questions, uncertainty and ambiguity has enabled me to hang on and continue the journey.

I have always had an admiration for the great explorers, those who risked their lives to explore new territories and countries. At the end of the twentieth century there are few physical places unexplored but there is a vast terrain of the spirit. We are challenged in that realm as never before because of the close proximity of people of different faith traditions. I do not think that we can ignore facing the questions raised by that challenge without seriously damaging our humanity. If we respond by an attempt to pull up the mental drawbridge and protect ourselves from those who are different, retreat into our groups of 'people like us' convinced that we are right and our world view is the only one, we will be condemning ourselves to a very impoverished future, for we will be refusing to grow. History shows us how destructive that attitude can be. As we approach the new millennium we need to remember our history, reflect on the outcomes and learn from the process if we are not simply going to go on repeating the same mistakes.

Life is a journey and the quest is to explore what it means to be human, and that is about our relationships with God, ourselves, each other and the environment. If we have the courage to be open on that journey we can find ourselves enriched by every life experience. God comes to us in all that happens. This book tells of how I have found myself enriched by the many friends I have met on that human journey, friends discovered in unexpected places, who at first seemed to be very different but on deeper acquaintance displayed similar human aspirations, hopes and fears.

My own journey has taken an unexpected turn over the last few months and I know that the experience of the past eighteen years has given me the tools for discerning what is of God in the process. Most of the time in South London I was living alone on 'detached service'. I kept in regular contact with the Community of the Sacred Passion and visited the Mother House at Effingham most months. After seven years I sensed the need for a change and knew that if I was to continue as a member of the community I must return to convent life.

No one expected it to be an easy adjustment and when I came to live in the convent at Effingham in November 1997 my sisters were very generous in their welcome and help to smooth the transition period. At first it felt like coming home and I delighted in the silence and regular pattern of prayer. The building of the new wing for our elderly sisters had just been completed and there was an air of hope and possibility of change. I could see great possibilities for the use of the beautiful refectory in the new wing. As we became less able to go out into the world to pursue our missionary vocation could we allow the world to come to us? I was very grateful for the space to explore which I had been given in South London. I had gained a great deal from it and now I wanted to be generous in sharing the fruits of that experience with my sisters.

It was not long before I was feeling very bereft without my friends of other faith traditions and cultures. For eighteen years I had lived in a multiracial, multicultural world and before that I had spent fifteen years in Africa. Now in this particular part of Surrey I suffered a real cultural shock. I began to explore the possibility of work in Epsom and following up contacts I was able to meet with the Epsom and Ewell Islamic Society and the Mauritian Hindu Sabha (society). These groups did not have their own premises and met in each other's houses or in St Barnabas church hall for festivals and special occasions. The after-school teaching for Muslim children was held in a hall at St Ebba's hospital with a teacher from the Azhor Academy in Norbury, Maulana Ishmael. When I visited this group and met the Maulana I was delighted to discover that he knew Maulana Sikander from Balham Mosque. I sent my greetings and already I was beginning to feel connected again.

The vicar of St Barnabas Church had given me these contacts and a great deal of information about Epsom. He gave me the name of Serena Powis, an officer at the town hall who was secretary to the recently formed Ethnic Minorities Working Party. Through her I got more valuable information and learnt something of the diversity of the population in the borough of Epsom and Ewell. Recent research had revealed that there were at least thirty-eight languages spoken in the borough and that one of the wards in Ewell had an ethnic minority population of eleven per cent. These people had been recruited for the local hospitals and although some of those hospitals were closing, many of the people had settled, married and had children. It was interesting to note that almost none of those children became nurses when they grew up. Their parents expected something better for them.

Serena was most interested in my background and invited me to join the working party. I was delighted to do so but soon found that this was going to be a far greater challenge than anything I had so far encountered. The ethnic minority population was very diverse, it was misleading to talk about ethnic communities, more often it was a case of a few families. How were we to contact them, communicate effectively and enable them to make use of local authority services?

At Effingham almost all the sisters attended the local parish church on a Sunday. There we were made to feel very welcome and some sisters were involved in the life and activities of the parish. It seemed a pity not to spread ourselves a bit more

widely but transport was a problem. However I did have the use
of a Honda 90, exchanged for the old Honda 70 a year or two
ago, a bit heavier and faster but I do not have the same affection for it as I had for the old one. I contacted the Revd David
Eaton, vicar of St Mary and St Nicholas, Leatherhead, and discussed the possibility of being associated with the parish. David
was very welcoming and I started to attend the parish church on
Sundays. I was warmly accepted by the members of the church
and soon felt very much at home. The congregation was very
mixed in social background and residents from Seeability with
severe disabilities were very important members of the congregation. One of the great bonuses for me has been the evident
integration of people with serious disabilities into the life of the
town. I am impressed by the quality of life they are enabled to
have and they always have interesting stories to tell of their out-
ings and activities. I get a sense of a very caring community, able
to celebrate and enjoy life, and I find that a real inspiration.

Life in Leatherhead and Epsom was very creative and
energizing but life at the convent was becoming more and more
difficult. I became increasingly aware of the dissatisfaction of
many of my sisters because I was out so much. I felt frustrated
and undervalued. We were founded as a missionary order
and now most of our energy was going into looking after ourselves. The order I had joined in 1968 had changed beyond
recognition. In an aging community the struggle to cope with
the practical demands of daily life was grinding us down and
reducing our perceptions. There seemed little place for vision
and our community life suffered accordingly. We were having
to live a life for which we had not been trained and for which
some of us had no vocation. I had never had to live so much
convent life. The moment I had received the habit as a novice I
was sent to work in the Hospital and Homes of St Giles at East
Hanningfield and I have been working outside the convent ever
since. The life of the past eighteen years in Walsall and South
London had certainly not prepared me for the convent life I was
being asked to live at Effingham.

I slowly and reluctantly became aware that I was temperamentally unsuited for convent life and was therefore probably in the wrong place. This was such a desperately hard thing to admit and took several months of agonizing before I could do so. After nine months at the convent I became aware that my mental and physical health was under threat, too much energy was going into coping with the frustrations of convent life and this meant that my ministry was suffering. I was forced to own that I was deeply unhappy and I did not believe that was God's will for me.

During the time I was living alone in London I had became aware that I did have a contemplative vocation and it was probably this unacknowledged awareness which drew me to test my vocation as a religious sister thirty years ago. I had considered that a contemplative vocation was something for special, holy people, not for earthy, fragile Maureen. It was while living alone, particularly at a very stressful time of my life, that I learned to befriend my loneliness and out of that came a love of solitude and a deeper relationship with the Risen Christ. The heart of my life was that relationship with the One who understood and accepted me wholly with all my frailty and pigheadedness as well as my goodness and giftedness. I learned that the greatest gift God has given me is my own personhood, into the creation of which he invites my co-operation. I began to learn what it means to love myself and rejoice in my life experience which was increasingly opening up to new horizons. A constant refrain that ran through my mind was the call to choose life.

So at this devastatingly painful stage of my life I had to discern what choosing life meant for me. Was my unhappiness merely an extension of my mid-life crisis? (which I still maintain is a very good thing to have). As I approached sixty was I wanting an easier life, not this awful physical slog that would go on until I died or became physically incapable? How could I leave my sisters in the lurch when I owed them so much? I had made life vows in 1975 and I took them very seriously, regarding them like marriage vows – for better, for worse, for richer, for poorer, in sickness or in health. Now that my community had reached such a difficult period in its life how could I turn my back on it? I gradually became aware that part of me was dying and that an attempt to persevere in the wrong place would mean emotional and spiritual suicide.

Someone in whom I confided asked me to consider what I was most afraid of losing. Subsequent reflection quickly revealed that clinging to status and security was making me hang on. I came to a point where I shut myself in my room and simply stayed with the pain and confusion. I hardly knew if I prayed, maybe the odd 'Lord help, show me the way'. After about an hour and a half the turmoil settled and it seemed as if the decision was made in me. I had to explore my options. I started pushing doors, exploring very tentatively, first with David about the possibility of living and working in Leatherhead and then asking permission of my local bishop to live as a solitary under vows. The primary emphasis would be the contemplative life amongst people continuing my ministry in the local community. I had became aware that I did not need the cloister to live the contemplative life, indeed I was temperamentally more suited to living it in the wider community. The process of establishing a reasonable financial footing and finding suitable accommodation just rolled. I could hardly believe how smoothly it happened, more quickly than I felt able to keep up with emotionally at times. I kept thinking as each hurdle was passed, 'I can't believe that I am doing this. Soon there is going to be no turning back.'

The hardest part was taking leave of my sisters. Inevitably there was a great deal of pain and misunderstanding. This move I am experiencing as the most costly obedience so far in my life and yet the most liberating. In seeking release from my vows with CSP I am no longer regarded as a religious sister. Yet, newly settled in Leatherhead I am conscious of no break in my vocation. There is a seamlessness in my experience. The whole process has had a very focussing effect upon me, showing me what is most important in life and giving me the courage to go for it.

At the moment my new life is very embryonic. I recently

heard of a rabbinic saying, 'When you are going to do something new for God keep it under your heart for nine months.' This is exactly what I have done. I was at the convent for nine months before I made the decision, then came the month of very painful labour before the birth into my new life. What it means is unknown. I am to make new vows to my local bishop who is being wonderfully supportive and investigating what form those vows should take. There is sense of rebirth and many signs of hope for the future as well as the pain and fear. Saying 'Yes' to God means embracing the whole of my life experience. My life feels all of a piece, a wonderful mosaic of experience and the hope of more to come with my increasing number of friends of all faith traditions and cultures. It is ironic that at the moment I am no longer recognized as part of a community I feel more in community than ever before. What form of the religious life will continue the charism of the prophetic tradition in the new millennium? What shape does community need to be? There is need for a variety of models and I would like to explore this with others.

A few weeks ago I joined old friends at a gathering celebrating One World Week at the South London Liberal Synagogue. It was a time of shared entertainment and reflection on the theme 'Shaping our Future'. This time I took part as a clown since over the past three years I have been exploring my journey by sacred clowning. I am no longer Sister Maureen, and I often feel very bereft with that loss of identity, but there is a whole new life of exploration ahead of me as I explore who Maureen is before God. What has been experienced as a very deep loss is also the threshold of another great adventure.

The journey goes on, the adventure of exploring this wonderful world God has given us and receiving the gift of the Kingdom. It has been for me a process of waking up. Jesus did not say 'Do this' or 'Don't do that'. He said '*Look*!' Look, the Kingdom is upon you. It is like a grain of mustard seed, which, although with tiny beginnings, will grow into a great tree. It is like the yeast in flour making bread, like treasure hidden in a field or the pearl of great price found by the dealer in precious stones. There is a sense of excitement, of surprise and delight. It is pure gift, under our very noses but we often cannot see because we are not looking.

Waking up can be painful. So often we prefer to remain asleep. Waking up means experiencing the pain as well as the joy of life, for they are inextricably linked. If we shut ourselves off from the pain of our lives, from the ambiguity and confusion of our complex and challenging modern world, from the challenge of those who have very different world views and belief systems we will make ourselves incapable of feeling the full joy and delight of life. Most of us live with our senses only half turned on. We miss so much of life because we do not look or listen. The human problem of self-centredness is reinforced by our failure to fully use our senses. There is such an exciting world out there if only we will turn our senses really on and look, listen, touch, taste and smell all that God wants to give us in this wonderful world.

This is the shape of the faith needed as we approach the new millennium. A faith that is open to all the challenges which come to us in our complex world. A faith that is intensely vulnerable and open to allow ourselves to be changed, a faith that recognizes God in the whole of our life experience, a faith free of that mental filing system which limits our perceptions and hinders our growth.

I have discovered a growing unity, trust and respect amongst people of many faith traditions. It is a movement which is gaining momentum. I have given examples of what I have seen. There are many people all over the country involved in similar ventures, courageously and patiently working away at developing good interfaith relationships and practical projects to improve quality of life in their locality. Where there is such working together God's Kingdom is welcomed and celebrated. The fruit of the Spirit is evident in the lives of a very diverse group of people. When we see God at work in the world, mission becomes exciting as we learn to co-operate with God. Christian mission is as much about being as doing, it is very ordinary and everyday, about neighbourliness and good citizenship. If we but open our eyes we will see the One at work who says, 'Behold, I am making all things new.' For the more we look, the more we shall see and the more we see God at work in the world, the more joy and hope will take hold of us and we shall learn to be the gospel.

Notes

Chapter 10

1. Frederick Buechner, *Wishful Thinking: A Theological ABC*, Harper and Row, New York 1973, p. 95; as quoted by M. Scott Peck in *A World Waiting to be Born*, Arrow 1994, p. 99.
2. John V. Taylor, *The Go-Between God*, SCM Press 1972.

Chapter 11

3. Donald Coggan, 'Christians and Jews', *Theology*, Vol. XCIII, July/August 1990, p. 262.

Chapter 13

4. *Siddur Lev Chadesh. Services and Prayers*, Union of Liberal and Progressive Synagogues 1995, pp. 567–70.

Chapter 15

5. Melvyn Matthews, *Delighting in God*, Collins Fount 1987, p. 21.

Chapter 16

6. Professor Kabal Singh, AMN, PJK, 'A Symbol of Sikh Solemnity', *Sikhism – Way of Life*, Vol. 1, 9, Spring 1993. Published by The Sikh Educational and Cultural Association.

7. Karbala. A leaflet produced by the Islamic Information Bureau and reproduced with permission.

Chapter 19

8. H. A.Williams, *True Resurrection*, Mitchell Beazley 1979, p. 53.
9. Here I am indebted to the work of the Revd Jim Cotter.